CHAMPIONSHIP COACHES

MIKE KRZYZEWSKI

JOHN FREDRIC EVANS

Enslow Publishing
101 W. 23rd Street
Suite 240
New York, NY 10011
USA
enslow.com

Published in 2020 by Enslow Publishing, LLC
101 W. 23rd Street, Suite 240, New York, NY 10011

Library of Congress Cataloging-in-Publication Data
Names: Evans, John Fredric, author.
Title: Mike Krzyzewski / John Fredric Evans.
Description: New York : Enslow Publishing, LLC, 2020. | Series: Championship Coaches | Includes bibliographical references and index. | Audience: Grades: 7-12.
Identifiers: LCCN 2018002102| ISBN 9780766098015 (library bound) | ISBN 9780766098022 (paperback)
Subjects: LCSH: Krzyzewski, Mike—Juvenile literature. | Basketball coaches—United States—Biography—Juvenile literature. | Duke University—Basketball—History—Juvenile literature. | Duke Blue Devils (Basketball team)—History—Juvenile literature.
Classification: LCC GV884.K79 E83 2019 | DDC 796.323092 [B] —dc23
LC record available at https://lccn.loc.gov/2018002102

Printed in China

To Our Readers: We have done our best to make sure all website addresses in this book were active and appropriate when we went to press. However, the author and the publisher have no control over and assume no liability for the material available on those websites or on any websites they may link to. Any comments or suggestions can be sent by email to customerservice@enslow.com.

Photo Credits: Cover, pp. 1, 83, 89 Andy Lyons/Getty Images; pp. 5, 87 Lance King/Getty Images; p. 9 Kirn Vintage Stock/Corbis Historical/Getty Images; p. 11 Nancy Kennedy/Shutterstock.com; p. 12 Bettmann/Getty Images; pp. 16, 28, 34, 41, 42, 49, 69 © AP Images; pp. 19, 25 Collegiate Images/Getty Images; pp. 23, 30 Focus on Sport/Getty Images; p. 46 Doug Pensinger/Getty Images; pp. 56, 62 Brian Bahr/Getty Images; p. 64 Timothy A. Clary/AFP/Getty Images; pp. 72, 75, 78 Streeter Lecka/Getty Images; p. 81 Jamie Squire/Getty Images; p. 92 Grant Halverson/Getty Images.

CONTENTS

INTRODUCTION

In sports the most obvious way to measure success is wins, and basketball coach Mike Krzyzewski has more than anyone. Krzyzewski, known to most as "Coach K," set the record for most wins way back in 2011, and in 2015 he became the first Division I men's basketball coach to win one thousand games. Another measure of merit is championship performance. Krzyzewski led his Duke Blue Devils to the NCAA title in 1991, 1992, 2001, 2010, and 2015, while his Olympic teams took home the gold all three times he was head coach. Among other awards, Krzyzewski was named Naismith College Coach of the Year three times and is a member of the Basketball Hall of Fame. You could also look at his program's graduation rate, which is annually elite. But to really understand the greatness of this coach and his more-than-forty-year career, you have to listen to his players.

"I count my blessings to have had the opportunity to spend four years at Duke with Coach [K]," said Shane Battier, who graduated in 2001. "During that time, I not only became a champion, I became a man."[1]

"His ability to connect and send the right message to players—the modern young college athlete—I think is why he has continued to be successful,"[2] Grant Hill said in 2015.

Coach K and his players celebrate Duke's 68–63 win over Wisconsin in the 2015 NCAA championship game.

"Anything he says, we trust,"[3] said Quinn Cook, who played four years for Krzyzewski.

Krzyzewski has been deified and crucified in equal measure by basketball fans who cheer both for and against Duke. Some say that ACC officials' whistles too often blow in Duke's favor, while others contend that this complaint produces the opposite result. "I do think sometimes the officiating goes the other way because guys are trying to prove that we *don't* get all the calls," said Coach K. "But if that's what comes with winning, I'll deal with it. It's better than losing and having everyone talk about what a bunch of great guys we are."[4]

Krzyzewski is not a coolly analytical leader; his instincts and his emotions, guide him. "I coach by feel," he said. "I follow my heart."[5]

His language can be profane, both on and off the court. In 1990, the *Durham Morning Herald* published a transcript of the coach blasting the staff of Duke's student newspaper for assigning "midterm grades" to his players—their fellow students—in an article. His intent was to remind the journalists that Duke's players were people too, but he was reprimanded for his crude language. In response, the coach apologized—and over time he would become far less fiery in demeanor—but it's fair to say his passion is undiminished.

A Krzyzewski team is talented, but his players are not always the greatest athletes in the nation. Their victories can generally be attributed to teamwork, poise, and heart. As he put it, "At Duke, we search for good kids with strong character—not necessarily kids with great talent who can play, but great individuals who are willing to be part of a team and who are coachable."[6]

The coach maintains a close, honest, and open relationship with his players. "I want you to believe me when I tell you that you are great *and* I want you to believe me when I tell you that you are not working hard enough,"[7] said Krzyzewski. But at the same time, his philosophy relieves the pressure on the individual and shifts it to the group. "Handling the responsibility for wins and losses together removes the burden from one individual's shoulders and distributes it among each member of the team," said Coach K. "Just imagine: what could you do if you believed you could not fail? Being on a team that embraces collective responsibility puts you in that position. You, individually, cannot fail. That atmosphere is conducive to high-level performance and places you and your team in the position to be bold and unafraid, and if you should lose, you are not alone."[8]

Though he coaches every team differently and has adapted along with the sport and the times, there are certain principles Krzyzewski will never abandon. "I coach not to win or lose, I coach to have everybody on the same page with heart, mind and soul. And if it can't happen, then I don't want to coach."[9] Winning is a side effect of what he wants to accomplish. "The game is important, unbelievably important, because it's people stuff," Coach K told *Sports Illustrated* in 1992. "But whether or not we beat Vegas isn't unbelievably important. If we do it, it's usually the result of some really neat things. If you've given everything and lost, you should feel good."[10]

That's one good feeling he isn't well-acquainted with.

1

WORKING-CLASS ORIGINS AND ARMY DISCIPLINE

Mike Krzyzewski (pronounced *shih ZHEF skee*) was born in 1947 in Illinois. His parents, Bill and Emily, were Polish immigrants who started their family in a well-maintained corner of inner-city Chicago. They shared a small home with Mike's aunt, uncle, and cousins. For twenty-five years, his father was an elevator operator before buying a local tavern. Mike's mother had only an eighth-grade education and worked nights scrubbing floors at the Chicago Athletic Club. As Mike would later put it, "I had the benefit of learning at an early age that some of the greatest people in the world clean floors for a living."[1] His deep friendship with a custodian at Duke, D. C. Williams, began because Coach K has as much respect for that profession as any.

Growing up, Mike was known as "Mick" among his peers. His best buddy as a kid was Dennis "Moe" Mlynski, and they would remain lifelong friends. While the local community center was a haven for the boys, the area lacked Little League, Pop Warner, or other group sports. So, Krzyzewski took the initiative and put together games for everyone. "My passion has been for teaching and coaching from the

The Polish National Alliance sponsored boys' basketball teams like this 1943 squad. In his neighborhood, a young Krzyzewski had to organize games himself.

days when I organized my buddies into teams in a Chicago schoolyard,"[2] Coach K remembered.

This was also the setting for more solitary play, as a young Mike would practice his skills with nothing more than a net and a ball. "I can remember playing basketball, all alone," he wrote in his book *Beyond Basketball*. "I would take jump shots, drive to the hoop for layups, shoot free throws, all the while verbalizing a running commentary of the game I was playing in my head. 'Down by one ... 79–78 ... six seconds on the clock ... Krzyzewski dribbling down the court, crosses over ... Three ...Two ... One!'"[3]

In his imagination, Mike believed that he was really in the big game with a chance to be the hero. If his shot went in, he celebrated the win. If it didn't, there was always a foul on the play that sent him to the free throw line. "Though I enacted a broad range of imaginary scenarios throughout my youth, one thing remained the same: when I imagined, I always won!"[4]

> ***"Throughout my life, my mom has been the person that I've always looked up to."***[5]
>
> **—Mike Krzyzewski**

Coach K's family's faith charted the early course of his life. "I grew up in a very strict Catholic family and attended Catholic boy's school all my life,"[6] he recounted. Mike's parents also instilled in him the idea that anything he did was his, and he had to take ownership of it. "Michael, everything you do has your personal signature on it," said Emily, his mother. "You should take

The imposing West Point campus as seen from across the Hudson River in Garrison, NY. After high school, Krzyzewski was reluctant to accept his appointment, but it was a truly formative experience for the future legend.

pride in it because it's yours."[7] She took pride in something as simple as a batch of her famous chocolate chip cookies. When money was tight, each one got three chocolate chips. But even then, if a cookie had only two chips in it, that wasn't good enough and she'd throw it out. To this day, Coach K believes we shouldn't take pride in trophies or accolades, but in doing something the very best way we can.

Mike soon became one of Archbishop Weber High School's star players and twice led the Chicago's Catholic league in scoring. The feisty guard received recruiting attention from Wisconsin and Creighton, but it was an offer from Coach Bobby Knight, the head basketball coach at the United States Military Academy, that would change the course of his life. Mike was honored by the offer and wanted to play basketball

Early in his career, Bobby Knight was one of the most combustible coaches in the game, but his hot temper masked a great strategic mind.

for Knight, but he had no interest in joining the Army. At that point, Mike's aspirations were to teach high school and coach basketball there, so he planned to decline Knight's offer.

His parents didn't endorse this decision. After an animated conversation in Polish, which Mike had never learned, they presented him with a united front. They were convinced that the formal education he would receive at West Point was a great opportunity for him. And besides, they didn't have the money to pay for a traditional college education. "I went, I think, because of my parents," wrote Coach K in his book *Leading with the Heart*. "They had never steered me wrong before. I was on a great team even back then, although I didn't completely appreciate it at the time."[8]

"A cadet will not lie, cheat or steal—or tolerate those who do."

— West Point cadet honor code

MILITARY PRECISION

After accepting his appointment to the Academy in 1965, Mike wanted to quit many times but couldn't bring himself to let his parents down. "My first real experience with failure came when I went to West Point," he said. "There, failure was a common occurrence for me."[9] Coming from the big city, Mike couldn't tie a knot, put up a tent, or even swim. This put him behind from the start. What the academy called "Summer Orientation," the cadets called "Beast Barracks," because the training was so intense. It tested Mike to the utmost.

One incident that made a big impression on him occurred early in his four years at Army. He was walking across a field with his roommate when the kid stepped in a puddle, spattering mud on Mike's shoes. Soon thereafter the two "plebes" were stopped by stern upperclassmen who saw the muddy shoes and gave Mike demerits for this uniform infraction. Initially, Mike blamed his roommate. It wasn't Mike's fault

The General Leads

With 902 wins, Bobby Knight set a record in NCAA Division I competition, but his former player and assistant coach Mike Krzyzewski would later shatter this mark. Unlike Coach K, "The General" was known for his hot temper and famously tossed a chair across the court in a 1985 loss to Purdue. Knight led the Indiana Hoosiers to three NCAA championships, including an undefeated season in 1975–76. They were the last men's team to go undefeated all the way to a national title. In 1984, Knight became one of only three coaches to win NCAA, NIT, and Olympic finals when his team took gold at the Los Angeles Summer Games.

his shoes were muddy! But later he realized that he should have gone straight back to the dorm to deal with his shoes. He chose not to and that, in fact, was why he'd gotten in trouble. He would later tell this story to his players as a lesson in personal responsibility.

Another meaningful moment came when Mike and his two roommates failed a test that involved lining up in formation, returning to their barracks to change uniforms, and getting back in formation within two minutes. If one roommate was late, all three were considered late. By the third time around they knew they needed to work together to get dressed in time. After several practice runs, when the time came, the cadets helped each other get into full dress uniform and made it back outside in under two minutes. "We learned to depend on one another, which, in turn, made us better," said Coach K. "Through that experience, and many others like it, we learned that failure is just part of success. If you fall down, you get up. If your tent falls down, you put it up again."[10]

"Every Cadet an Athlete"

In 1802, President Thomas Jefferson called for the establishment of the United States Military Academy at West Point, where a fort was already located. Built on high ground with a scenic view of the Hudson River, the Army campus sits fifty miles (80 kilometers) north of New York City. For students (cadets), participation in competitive sports is required and Army maintains a fierce rivalry with the US Naval Academy. Students' tuition is fully funded in exchange for active duty service after graduating with a bachelor of science degree. Most who complete the forty-seven-month program are commissioned as second lieutenants in the US Army.

Mike also grew to admire the West Point honor code: "A cadet will not lie, cheat or steal—or tolerate those who do." Establishing a culture of honesty and truth-telling is something Coach K would try to do with every team he led.

Meanwhile, Mike excelled at athletics. In his three seasons on Knight's Army team, the Cadets compiled a 51–23 record and twice paced the country in fewest points allowed on defense. Bobby Cremins, the former South Carolina player and Georgia Tech coach, said this about his rival, Mike Krzyzewski: "He was a tough, aggressive-type player."[11]

In Mike's junior year, the Cadets qualified for the National Invitational Tournament (NIT), a prestigious competition at that time. By his senior year in 1969, Mike was the team captain. Soon after earning the game ball for a big win over Navy, he received tragic news. His father had died of a sudden brain hemorrhage. Coach Knight not only drove Mike to the airport, he flew out later in the evening to support the family.

The team had two games remaining, with another spot in the NIT at stake. With no pressure from Knight, Mike made sure he came back in time to help the team win both games. In the NIT quarterfinals, he shut down South Carolina's All-American guard John Roche and Army pulled off a major upset. The team finished fourth in the tournament, quite an accomplishment for a service academy.

On the very day he graduated from West Point, Mike Krzyzewski married Carol "Mickie" Marsh in the academy's Catholic chapel.

In the 1969 NIT, South Carolina star John Roche (*shooting*) discovered that Krzyzewski (*arms up*) played excellent "D." Krzyzewski had learned the fundamentals he would instill in his own players.

Introduced by a mutual friend, they had met and gone dancing two years earlier, during one of Mike's visits home. The cocky cadet told her in their second meeting—a Chicago Bears game—that she was his third choice for a date that night. This infuriated Mickie, but his quirky confidence and the nine roses he gave her earned Mike another shot. "Of course, I was determined to never be his third choice again," she later said. "But … It made me want to know him that much more. He believed that whatever the consequences were of telling me the truth, they were less painful than lying to me."[12]

Almost fifty years later, Mike would tell you he feels very fortunate that his bravado didn't blow it for him. In Mickie he found his life partner and pillar of strength.

2

SPECIAL K

After graduation, Krzyzewski's first assignment was as a field artillery officer at Fort Carson, in Colorado. By 1971, it looked as though he was going to serve in Vietnam, but when the time came, he was sent to Korea instead. He later expressed the view that the government was never committed to winning the war in Vietnam, and that it had betrayed the commitment of all the US troops who died there. "I have friends with whom I went to school who are buried at West Point cemetery," he wrote in *Leading with the Heart*. "I'll never forget that. So if I ask an eighteen-year-old on my team for his full commitment, I'm going to make certain that wherever I'm leading him, both the destination and the journey will be worthy."[1]

For five years, Coach K fulfilled his military obligations and served abroad. Of course, basketball still found its way into his life. For three years, he coached teams at Army bases before becoming the head coach at the West Point prep school in Belvoir, Virginia, a post he held for two years.

In 1974, Coach K was a twenty-seven-year-old Army captain with a four-year-old daughter, Debbie. By this time he had a feeling that coaching might be his calling, but he was far from certain. An opportunity came when he was offered a graduate assistant coaching position at the University of Indiana, where Bobby Knight was now the head coach. It was a difficult decision. Could he really walk away from the security an Army career offered?

Mike discussed it with Mickie, of course. "She has been my most important teammate throughout our marriage and career,"[2] said Coach K. The two decided Mike should take the Indiana position, so Mike resigned from the Army, and the Krzyzewskis became a basketball coaching family. He was gone almost every weekend to recruit and Mickie worked at a local bank to supplement their income.

Even after coaching Mike for three years in college and hiring him as an assistant coach, Knight still couldn't pronounce his name and called him "Kre-shefski." When a reporter told him his pronunciation was off, Knight quipped, "It's not my fault if he pronounces his name wrong."[4]

> *[Failure] is a "stepping-stone on your journey to greatness."*[3]
>
> —Mike Krzyzewski

The assistants on Knight's staff, Henry Iba and Pete Newell, gave the newcomer a word of advice. They told Coach K to learn absolutely everything he could from Knight, but not to try to be him, or anyone else. They suggested that he take what he learned and fit it into who he was as a person, leader, and coach. "Essentially, they told me to be myself,"[5] concluded Mike.

He took their advice to heart and soon blazed his own bold trail. Still, Knight was a fine mentor. "I learned a great deal about organization and preparation from Coach Knight," Mike said. "Success is not a matter of just wanting to win. It's a matter of preparing to win—which is much more important. Now if you can combine the two, you're on the right road."[6]

Krzyzewski (*left*) and Bobby Knight have had some ups and downs in the course of their six-decade relationship, but they've always supported each other in tough times.

The Hoosiers went undefeated that year (1975) until losing in the NCAA Tournament's Regional Final. Indiana's star forward, Scott May, had broken his leg in February. By the time of the tournament, his leg had healed, but neither he nor the team had been able to reach the level of play they'd displayed before his accident.

The next year, Indiana again went undefeated with a healthy Scott May, but this time their tournament run ended in a national championship. With Bobby Knight's recommendation, Mike had already become the head coach at West Point, but, he knew he wouldn't be there forever. "I loved coaching at my alma mater, but deep down I knew I wanted to do what Coach Knight had done: take a team to the Final Four and win a national championship,"[7] said Mike.

He knew that wouldn't be possible at Army, which didn't have the recruiting power of a traditional college. After all, potential NBA prospects don't want to graduate with five years in the Army ahead of them. After a handful of fairly successful seasons—under Krzyzewski's leadership, a previously 3–22 team compiled a 73–59 record and even received an NIT invite in 1978—a big opportunity came when Duke's athletic director, Tom Butters, interviewed him in 1980. "It was obvious to me that Mike's teams were well-coached, organized, intense competitors,"[8] recalled Steve Vacendak, who in helping Butters assess coaching candidates brought Coach K to his attention. Vacendak also liked that Krzyzewski was undaunted by Duke's high admissions standards, an obstacle in recruiting that seemed insignificant compared to those he faced at Army.

Though Butters was equally impressed, he knew it was a stretch to hire the thirty-three-year-old coach. He later confessed to thinking, "How did I justify hiring a coach who had just gone 9–17 at *Army* to coach an ACC team that had just played in the final eight?"[9] Still, Butters felt certain this man would be a great coach. "I had a list of things that are important to me in hiring anyone and he met, in every way, all of those, at the highest level."[10] Butters spoke to Bob Knight about his former protégé, getting this compelling endorsement: "Mike Krzyzewski has all of my good qualities and none of my bad."[11]

Coach K felt so strongly that Duke was the right place for him that he turned down another good job, at Iowa State, without having yet secured the position in Durham. After three interviews, with Butters' gut and Vacendak telling him to take a chance on Coach K, the athletic director hired him to coach the Duke basketball team.

The hiring shocked most observers, including the local media. An ACC school hiring the West Point coach? Krzyzewski wasn't even an alum! Sophomore guard Vice Taylor's response to the news was, "What the [heck] is a Krzyzewski?"[12] Asked about his last name, the new coach quipped, "It was a lot worse before I changed it."[13]

WINS WERE HARD TO COME BY

In Mike's first year, 1981, Duke went 17–10. Meanwhile, ten miles away, their in-state rivals, the North Carolina Tar Heels, were dominating. Led by legendary coach Dean Smith, the Tar Heels narrowly missed the national championship that year after losing to Indiana, and in

Foster Care

When Bill Foster was named head coach at Duke in 1974, he took over a program in shambles. The team was coming off the worst season in its history and played in the nation's toughest conference, the ACC. Four years later, Foster's recruits won the ACC Tournament and stormed the NCAA Tournament, making it to the championships before they were felled by Kentucky. Coach K has said that every member of his first great recruiting class told him they had memories of Foster's '78 team, which put Duke on the map. Krzyzewski believes that he couldn't have signed them if it weren't for Foster's foundation.

1982 they won it all, aided by a talented freshman named Michael Jordan. And Duke? In Coach K's second year, the Blue Devils posted a 10–17 record, their worst ever. The win total inched up to eleven the next year as another ACC rival, Jim Valvano's North Carolina State Wolfpack, won the 1983 national championship.

"Had I known what the first three years were going to be like, I might have thought twice [about taking the job]"[14] Krzyzewski reflected, years later. He also confessed to feeling significant self-doubt as his ACC rivals dominated the Final Four. For the first time, Coach K wondered if his dream of competing at the highest level would ever be realized.

However, Krzyzewski's recruiting class for the 1982–83 season clearly had the potential to be special. Freshmen Mark Alarie, Jay Bilas, Johnny Dawkins, and David Henderson were far better than the team's record indicated, but they needed time to develop their talents. Losing to Virginia by 43 points in the ACC Tournament ended the season with a whimper.

The Man Behind the V Foundation

North Carolina State coach Jim Valvano had not only the gift of gab but also an exuberant spirit that was immortalized by his joyous celebration after the Wolfpack won the 1983 NCAA title. North Carolina State shocked the Houston Cougars with a buzzer-beating dunk in one of the greatest upsets in college basketball history. After being diagnosed with cancer at age forty-six, Valvano spoke the words "Don't give up, don't ever give up" in one of two powerful speeches delivered just weeks before his death in 1993. Another Valvano quote, "Take time every day to laugh, to think, to cry," was engraved on his tombstone.

The great Jim Valvano was known for his passionate personality. It made the North Carolina State coach a spell-binding public speaker, and Valvano helped an initially awkward Krzyzewski become quite good at it himself.

For the 1983–84 season, Krzyzewski added freshman point guard Tommy Amaker. Duke went 24–10 and beat Michael Jordan and the Tar Heels in the ACC Tournament semifinals. The victory announced that Duke was again a force to be reckoned with. Coach K and Dean Smith would be rivals for seventeen years, with many memorable duels between them. For the first time, Coach K had led a team to the NCAA Tournament, though the Final Four still seemed a distant goal.

The next season saw Duke go 23–8 and secure two NCAA Tournament wins. By 1985–86, Coach K's star recruits were seasoned and mature. Dawkins led the team in scoring, Amaker distributed the ball and played lockdown defense, and everyone else chipped in to make the team well rounded. Coach K honed his skill at keeping his players in the moment and not distracted by the previous play. Scorers are particularly prone to shooting slumps, so he learned how to encourage Dawkins to keep firing them up there. "If Johnny Dawkins missed four shots in a row during a key game, I would call him over and say something to him. Johnny, next time down, I want you to take another shot. Be confident. You're going to make the next shot,"[16] said Krzyzewski.

> ***"Having a positive influence on people, helping others; that's winning."***[15]
>
> **—Mike Krzyzewski**

The combination of good coaching and talented players hitting their stride produced a 37–3 record, an ACC title, a number-one ranking in the polls, and a trip to the NCAA championship game …

Mark Alarie (#32) and Coach K's superb 1982 recruiting class became the backbone of his roster in 1985.

which Duke then lost, 72–69, to Louisville. "If there is a game in my career I look back on with regret, it's that one,"[17] Coach K said. He didn't think he'd done enough to get his team ready to play. He also wished he'd played reserves more in the first half, keeping his four stars fresh enough for the finish. For example, if Krzyzewski had given more minutes to freshman guard Quin Snyder, maybe Amaker wouldn't have run out of gas in the fourth quarter. "If anyone came up short, it was me,"[18] concluded Coach K.

Regardless, getting to the threshold of a national championship was a tremendous accomplishment for the team. By reaching the Final Four, Coach K had achieved his first goal, and now he had his sights set on the next: a national title.

3

CLOSING IN ON A CHAMPIONSHIP, ONE STEP AT A TIME

By this point, it was clear that Tom Butters had bet on the right coach. More importantly, he'd stuck by him, even as Krzyzewski went 38–47 in his first three seasons. "It is easy to be committed to someone or something during good times, because when you are winning your commitment is never challenged," said Coach K. "But loyalty and dedication during more difficult times can be tough. Tom never wavered."[1]

Now the school was reaping the benefits. After Duke's appearance in the 1986 title game, the team made the Sweet Sixteen the following year. A key contributor was Danny Ferry, Krzyzewski's top recruit of the era and winner of several national Player of the Year awards. In 1988, Ferry set a Duke record for the highest number of points scored in a single game, with fifty-eight total. He helped the Blue Devils reach the Final Four that year, where Danny Manning and the Kansas Jayhawks bested them en route to a surprising national championship.

Tommy Amaker had recently returned, now a member of the coaching staff. Even back then, Coach K thought it important to have young assistants who could properly relate to the experience of current players. "I also like my former players around because they'll remember things I did years ago—and then remind me so I can employ those things again."[2] At various times, former players Quin Snyder, Johnny Dawkins, Steve Wojciechowski, and Jeff Capel would also join Coach K on the coaching side of the Duke bench.

The 1988–89 recruiting classes yielded two players who would become heroes of this storied program. Point guard Bobby Hurley was daring to the point of recklessness. He inspired his teammates to believe anything was possible, making Coach K's job much easier. Coach K tries to surround himself with people who radiate courage, and Hurley was one of those people. "Even when I felt stifled by moments of doubt, I could look into Bobby's eyes and find the confidence to proceed,"[4] said Krzyzewski. "Coaching Bobby, I learned to be more daring."[5]

> *"Don't worry about losing. Think about winning."*[3]
>
> —Coach K

In this 1989 NCAA Tournament game, Coach K waves to get his players' attention without yelling.

Center Christian Laettner was a sought-after recruit who had led his prep school to a pair of titles. In 1989, Laettner's freshman campaign, Duke played Arizona in a nail-biter. He was fouled with Duke trailing 77–75 and one second on the clock. His free throw attempt rimmed out; Arizona controlled the rebound; and the Blue Devils lost. Senior captains Ferry and Snyder were the first to console Laettner. "Danny [Ferry] had so much invested in that game," says Krzyzewski. "He was a senior. If Arizona won, Sean Elliott would get a leg up on Danny for Player of the Year. Yet Danny's first move was to go up to Christian and tell him it was all right, so Christian wouldn't feel he lost the game."[6]

This moment made Krzyzewski proud. Duke's culture of collective responsibility only strengthened their big-game mentality. "On a team that wins and loses together, there is no such thing as blame," said Coach K. "When somebody does something well, we all do it well. When somebody makes a mistake, we all make the mistake."[7] This philosophy makes players more confident because individuals don't carry the full burden of expectations on their shoulders. They're inspired to make plays, but aren't afraid they'll let others down if they fail.

The 1989–1990 season marked Duke's seventh straight appearance in the NCAA Tournament and fourth Final Four in five years, but they had yet to get over the hump and hoist a trophy. "Blame me," said Krzyzewski. "I'm the constant around here."[8] A joke made the rounds: "Why does Mike Krzyzewski quit after fourteen holes when he plays golf? Because he doesn't like the Final Four."[9] The coach could get a little snippy when the subject of winning it all came up. "There's no monkey on my back,"[10] he said repeatedly.

This year Coach K hoped to send out his seniors as champions. Duke made it to the NCAA final, but there they ran into trouble. Jerry Tarkanian's University of Nevada, Las Vegas (UNLV) Runnin' Rebels were a talented and mature team. On this occasion, they handed the Blue Devils a thirty-point loss, still the largest margin of defeat in title-game history. Krzyzewski was in awe of UNLV's performance. This was not a game that came down to Xs and Os, halftime adjustments, or mental mistakes. Asked what he would have done differently,

Laettner: Love Him or Hate Him?

Many opposing fans despised Christian Laettner, whether for his Ken doll looks, for stepping on a downed player in 1992, or for several clutch performances in the Big Dance. The player some called "The Blue Devil Himself" may have looked like a rich kid, but Laettner actually came from a working-class family and was no stranger to manual labor growing up. He enjoyed playing the heel, however, and says the hate only motivated him to play harder. Laettner was drafted third overall by the Minnesota Timberwolves and made the 1997 All-Star team as a member of the Atlanta Hawks.

he said, "Well, I could have showed up with a different team, or they could have had a different coach, or UNLV could have gotten sick."[11]

The Duke program was now 0–8 in Final Fours and 0–4 under Krzyzewski. After the game, Coach K remembers his mother telling him, "Don't worry! You'll do better next year." And he responded, "Mom, I know you're just trying to make me feel better. But you can't do a whole lot better than this. C'mon."[12]

That offseason, Grant Hill was a popular potential recruit with offers from a host of schools. But sitting in on the annual awards banquet at Duke convinced him this was a team culture he wanted to be a part of. Snyder, a departing senior, made an emotional speech

Christian Laettner (#32) reached four Final Fours, won a pair of titles, and hit last-second game-winners in two regional championship games. Clutch!

about the values he'd learned from Coach K: commitment, toughness, honesty, and integrity.

Despite Hill's freshman status, Coach K saw that the forward was so gifted he could contribute right away. Krzyzewski asked his stars to take Hill under their wing. He told them Hill would instinctively take a backseat to the upperclassmen, but he wanted them to make the kid feel like a key part of the team, right away. "By involving Hurley and Laettner, I was showing that I had a lot of confidence in both," said the coach. "And I knew they could bring Hill further along than just me working with him one on one."[13]

The friendship that developed between the three stars was special, but Coach K wants to see that happen with everyone. "Bonds have to form among *all* members of the team," he said. "Every individual must have a trusting relationship with every other member of the team."[14]

THEY SAID UNLV COULD NOT BE BEATEN

Entering the 1990–91 season, Krzyzewski told his team they were going to win the national championship. He'd never said that before and seldom would again. What made the statement even more remarkable was that he'd just lost Ferry to the NBA—to this day Ferry is the only Blue Devil to rank in the school's all-time top ten in the three key categories of points, rebounds, and assists. The team's one senior was a role player, Greg Koubek.

> *"Sometimes a loss can be a win."*[15]
>
> —Coach K

Nonetheless, the youngsters went 25–6 in the regular season—a perfect 16–0 at Cameron Indoor Stadium—and entered the NCAA Tournament as a No. 2 seed. There the team hit its stride, dispatching all four opponents by comfortable margins to qualify for another Final Four. To reach the championship game, however, they would have to avenge their season-ending defeat from a year earlier and oust the defending champions. Led by National Player of the Year Larry Johnson, UNLV had won forty-five games in a row. They hadn't even trailed in a game that year, winning by an average margin of twenty-five points without a single game decided in the final minute. All five starters were back from the team that had hammered Duke the previous March.

Still, Coach K harbored a quiet confidence, telling a friend, "We're good enough to stay close with them, and if it's close they won't know how to handle it because they haven't been in a close game all year."[16] His team was better than the year before, and they'd been in a lot of close games. To the media, Krzyzewski

No One Ran Like the Rebels

The Runnin' Rebels were named by their colorful coach, Jerry Tarkanian. UNLV's coach from 1973 to 1992, "Tark the Shark," lifted the program from obscurity to become a Division I program and then one of the highest-scoring teams in the nation. UNLV reached a quartet of Final Fours, with their success culminating in a 1990 win over Duke to take the national title. This team included future pros Stacey Augmon, Greg Anthony, and Larry Johnson, whose "Grandmama" persona in Converse commercials made him a household name before back injuries turned him into more of a complementary player than a star.

was more pessimistic, because he wanted the world—and potentially UNLV—to be certain of the outcome. He advised players to not even listen to what he said publicly. Meanwhile, behind closed doors, he made sure they felt, individually and as a group, that this was their time. He gave each player a video of his best individual plays throughout the season.

Remembering the lesson learned in 1986, Coach K rested Laettner at key junctures in the game. It was Hurley's turn to take charge. The playmaker had a certain look on his face, a look Krzyzewski knew and loved. It meant an opponents' physical play or the officials' calls could not rattle him. "Bobby Hurley was the leader of our team that day," said Krzyzewski. "He led with his daring heart."[17]

Every season, Coach K counts on players like Hurley to create chemistry and lift the team. Such a player makes him a better coach. "Leaders have to search for the heart on a team, because the person who has it can bring out the best in everybody else,"[18] said Krzyzewski.

Duke kept it close—they only trailed by two at halftime—and the second half saw seven straight lead changes as the teams traded baskets. Duke's smothering defense limited Larry Johnson to thirteen points, ten below his average. With two and a half minutes left to play, UNLV was up five with momentum on their side. Suddenly, Hurley sank a three-pointer. He hadn't looked over to see what his coach had wanted him to do; he had felt empowered to trust his instincts and take the initiative. "Most people think of game-winning shots as last-second shots," said Coach K. "That is not always the case. Bobby's courageous shot in the UNLV game is the perfect example."[19]

The basket seemed to shake the Runnin' Rebels' confidence and Duke tightened the screws defensively. The shot clock expired on UNLV. Then Hill found Brian Davis with a great pass, and the swingman's layup tied the game. With thirty seconds left, Duke had the ball. Their next shot went astray, but Laettner corralled the rebound and drew a foul. UNLV called timeout, and Krzyzewski's players joined him on the bench. Reminded of the Arizona game, he glanced at Laettner to gauge his readiness. "I got 'em, Coach," said the junior. "I got 'em."[20] He was smiling.

Bobby Hurley (#11, right) was named Player of the Game after Duke's 1991 win over Kansas in the championship game.

Laettner swished his foul shots to finish with 28 points. UNLV's desperate heave bounced into Hurley's hands, and the horn sounded. Duke had pulled one of the biggest upsets in Final Four history.

A last-moment letdown still seemed possible. Krzyzewski saw that his team was celebrating like this was the last game of the year, but it wasn't. Forty-eight hours later they would face a fine Kansas team, coached by Roy Williams, for the NCAA championship. This put one of Coach K's precepts to the test: win or lose, you must forget what happened yesterday and focus on tomorrow. Before practice, the team seemed far too casual, so he lit into them. "Only an ordinary team would be satisfied beating UNLV," he said. "But an ordinary team won't win tomorrow night—because an ordinary team cannot beat a great team."[21]

He then stormed out of the locker room. When he rejoined his players on the court he found them standing together, as a unit. Whatever they'd said to one another, it worked. He saw they weren't going to settle for second. Duke then secured a 72–65 win over Kansas to claim its first national championship. Laettner was named the tournament's Most Outstanding Player, and Coach K's mom could say "I told you so."

4

DUKE DID IT AGAIN

Mike Krzyzewski is very much aware that most seasons end with a loss. In his eyes, becoming national champions is not the only way a season can be successful. All he really cares about is that his team is constantly improving, getting one step closer to reaching its full potential. "When we win a game, everything isn't right. And when we lose a game, everything isn't wrong," he said. "If a team played as hard as they possibly could and came up short, did they really lose? I don't think so. I believe that any team that does its best is a winner ... A real winning attitude is about standards of excellence—which are variable from year to year, from team to team."[1]

Reaching the Final Four is, for Krzyzewski, as much as anyone should hope for. "I'd rather play and be beaten than not be there at

> *"I don't think we surprise people. We try to out-execute them."*[2]
>
> —Coach K

all,"[3] said the coach. "No coach should feel pressure when his team is in the Final Four."[4]

When tournament time comes, Coach K tells the team they're zero and zero—no wins, no losses. It's as though the season has begun all over again. "There's a finality to the NCAA Tournament," he tells his players. "If you lose, there is no other game. I don't know if that scares you or excites you. Either way, it's reality."[5] To cope with this reality, he wants them to stay loose. He's been known to take his team out of the gym to relax in the spring sunshine and savor the fact that they're still playing basketball in March. "I think you stress having fun and playing together and attacking. Not playing conservative. You can't be afraid to lose in the NCAAs."[6]

To remind the team what they're capable of, Krzyzewski likes to put together highlight reels of the season's best plays, with clips of the

From Floor General to Head Coach

New Jersey native Bobby Hurley led St. Anthony High School to a staggering 115–5 record before playing for Mike Krzyzewski at Duke, where he racked up an NCAA record 1,076 assists. In 1993 the Sacramento Kings drafted Hurley seventh overall, but early in his rookie year he suffered near-fatal injuries in a car accident. He has said his career would have been longer and more productive were it not for this setback. Now a coach, Hurley took over the Arizona State Sun Devils in 2015. The team opened the 2017–18 season 12–0, good for a number-three ranking nationwide (one spot ahead of Duke).

guys making great offensive and defensive efforts, diving for loose balls, and taking charges. "The idea is to put the players in a confident and positive frame of mind so they will be prepared for the first round of the tournament."[7]

Entering the 1991–92 season, Duke still had its terrific trio of Hurley, Laettner, and Hill. Krzyzewski didn't want his team to think of themselves as "defending champions," telling them, "We have to go out and earn everything we get. We are not *defending* anything. We are *pursuing* a national championship. *Pursuing!*"[8] He understands it's much more difficult to stay on top than to get there the first time.

Duke entered the year ranked number one and reeled off seventeen straight wins before suffering defeat against Dean Smith's Tar Heels. Duke only dropped one game the rest of the way, however. The Blue Devils closed the regular season 25–2, won the ACC, and entered the NCAA Tournament as a top seed.

THE FINAL SECONDS WILL NEVER BE FORGOTTEN

On March 28, 1992, a full crowd assembled at the Philadelphia Spectrum for perhaps the greatest college basketball game ever played. Duke met the Kentucky Wildcats in the regional finals, with a spot in the Final Four at stake. Coached by Rick Pitino, Kentucky had a battle-tested roster and a super sophomore in Jamal Mashburn, who would be taken fourth overall in the 1993 NBA Draft.

The game was tied 20–20 when the Blue Devils made a run and pushed to a 50–45 advantage at the break. Pushing their lead to as many as twelve points, Duke seemed as though they were headed for a commanding victory. But the veteran Wildcats hung tough. Mashburn sparked a furious rally and the game went to overtime, score knotted at 93.

The lead went back and forth until 7.8 seconds remained and Krzyzewski's team clung to a one-point lead. After a timeout, Kentucky took a tough shot in the teeth of Duke's always-disciplined defense. The ball banked in off the backboard. Now trailing 103–102, the Blue Devils would need a miracle of their own. They had 2.1 seconds to move the ball from one end of the court to the other and score. Calling timeout, Coach K could tell his team was stunned, every player's mind processing this cruel twist of fate. "In a crisis situation like this, I instinctively realized that I had to get them to snap out of the daze they were in, and I had to make them believe, positively, that they could win this game,"[9] said Krzyzewski.

So he met them leaving the court and, without hesitation, said "We're going to win!" twice. Ushering them to the bench, he repeated this twice more, later likening it to a verbal defibrillator shocking their hearts back to life. It worked, too, as he saw their eyes losing the glaze of shock. Everyone focused on their collective goal. Coach K asked Grant Hill if he could pass the ball seventy-five feet (twenty-three meters) to Laettner, who would be positioned at the opposite free throw line. Yes, he could. Could Laettner catch it and get off a shot in time? The answer was again yes. The players heard confidence in Hill and Laettner's responses. By breaking this daunting series of obstacles into individual parts, each player's responsibility became simple and concrete. Each player could focus on his own goal and have confidence he would achieve it while trusting that the others would do the same. "We left that huddle feeling like we would be winners,"[10] said Krzyzewski.

The play went exactly as diagrammed, beginning with Hill inbounding the ball to Laettner. "It was like a beautiful pass in football with the receiver in motion and the quarterback putting it right on the money, right where he knew his teammate would be,"[11] reflected Coach K.

Laettner dribbled, turned and uncorked a jump shot as the digits on the clock hit double-zero. As the ball slid through the net, Krzyzewski's eyes were on Laettner's face. The expression he found there told him the shot would be good. "I've seen Christian shoot so much," Coach K said, "that when I saw the arc, I knew it was in."[12]

Krzyzewski's first move, as pandemonium broke out on the court, was to go console Richie Farmer, a Kentucky senior playing his final game in a Wildcat uniform. But Duke had won, 104–103, and Laettner had proven himself one of the best clutch players in the college game. His missed free throw against Arizona was forgotten, though the lesson he learned that day lives on in Duke lore. A Blue Devil isn't afraid to let his teammates down; he's only eager to lift them up.

Coach K shook hands with Pitino and went to the press table to speak on the air with the Kentucky play-by-play announcer. "Please, be proud of your team," he told all the dejected Wildcat fans. "Give them the welcome home they deserve. They've represented you in the best possible way."[13]

Michigan's "Fab Five" fired the imaginations of fans as few teams do. Their legacy is built on an influential look and style, not the championships many predicted.

That day Laettner was flawless from the field and the stripe, going ten-for-ten and ten-for-ten (thirty-one total points). The only F on his report card was for sportsmanship, as he received a technical foul for stomping on a downed player, Aminu Timberlake, in retaliation for a hard shove out-of-bounds absorbed on the other end of the floor. "It was a dumb thing to do, but sometimes the emotion of the game gets into your head,"[14] said Laettner. (In 2015, he apologized.)

In the Final Four, Duke squared off against Indiana. Bob Knight's boys gave them everything they could handle, but Duke's defensive clampdown in the second half carried the day. The Blue Devils were back in the championship game. Their opponents, the Michigan

The bench goes wild as Duke closes out Michigan to win a second-straight title in 1992. They were the first champions to repeat since UCLA did it in 1973.

Wolverines, started five freshmen. Known as the Fab Five, this gifted group made up for their inexperience with raw talent.

Meanwhile, Christian Laettner had been struggling since the exhausting Kentucky game. In the first half, he had just two rebounds and more turnovers (seven) than points (five). Laettner's struggle was a big reason why Michigan took a 31–30 lead into the half. Nothing Krzyzewski could say or do would snap his star out of this funk. Then, in the locker room, a fiery, frustrated Hurley demanded that his teammate get it going. This cut through Laettner's weariness, and he came out stronger in the second half.

> *"I think leadership is never singular. In a good organization, it's plural."*[15]
>
> **—Coach K**

With less than seven minutes left in the game, Duke led by three. During a timeout, Coach K called a play for Laettner. It didn't go as planned, but somehow the center improvised and got the ball in the bucket. Then he immediately got a steal and fired the ball to Hill, who scored on a drive. Duke's 23–6 run put the precocious Wolverines away. "I still believe that it was Bobby Hurley's outburst in the locker room at halftime that won that game for us,"[16] said Krzyzewski.

Laettner ended his Duke career with a number of NCAA Tournament records, including games played (23) and won (21), free throws made (142) and points scored (407). He is the only player in history to start in four Final Fours.

The Fab Five Went Far

In 1991, four out of the nation's top ten prospects went to Michigan. The Wolverines' recruiting class that year was one of the most heralded in hoops history. Their baggy shorts, playground swagger, and hip-hop style set a trend that swept the nation and, ultimately, the NBA. Though the group never won a national championship at Michigan, four out of five reached the next level. Jalen Rose led the NBA Pacers to the 2000 Finals, and Juwan Howard won two NBA championships with the Miami Heat. Chris Webber was a five-time All-Star whose jersey was retired by the Sacramento Kings.

5

THE UNDOING OF A DELICATE DYNASTY

Coach K is a big believer in simulations. He runs practices in such a way that players continually face game situations, gaining experience in every phase. Whatever the variables are—number of team fouls, time on the shot clock or game clock, etc.—they practice it. Sometimes he makes players shoot free throws in the middle of practice, when they're winded, to replicate a real game. He even has the team practice timeouts. Krzyzewski's thought is that if nothing feels unfamiliar, if players have been in every situation before, they won't be tense when it's time for the real thing.

This preparation produces tangible results. On multiple occasions Duke has made more free throws in a season than their opponents even attempted. The Blue Devils are experts at playing suffocating defense without fouling the opposition. "The worst thing we can do is put the [other] team in a one-and-one,"[1] said Krzyzewski.

The 1992–1993 edition of the Blue Devils was as well prepared as any. While they lacked the star-power of Laettner, Duke still had Hurley, Hill, and future NBA players Antonio Lang and Cherokee Parks. Nonetheless, their season came to an abrupt end in the second round of the NCAA Tournament when California's freshman point guard (and future NBA legend) Jason Kidd played lights-out in an upset win for the Golden Bears. Kidd's duel with Hurley was epic, as the Duke star hit six three-pointers and finished with thirty-two points, nine assists, and just one turnover.

It was tough for Coach K to come to grips with the graduation of Hurley and Thomas Hill, another Duke stalwart since 1990. In the locker room after the game, he embraced Hurley for more than a minute. "I wish you could feel what I feel," Krzyzewski told reporters. "It tears me up that we lost only because I don't have a chance to coach these two guys anymore. I've won for so long with these guys and I'll win for the rest of my life for having been associated with them."[3]

> ***"Courage means daring to do what you imagine."***[2]
>
> **—Coach K**

A much sadder event in 1993 was the death of Coach K's friend and former rival Jim Valvano. The two had become so close that Krzyzewski was at Valvano's bedside when he passed. "This six months or so I spent with him at the end were the best six months I've ever spent with another man," said Coach K. "He made me understand that life is precious."[4]

Duke had another strong year the following season, but with a thinner roster than in years past, the Blue Devils weren't expected to make a deep run in the NCAA Tournament. It was a surprise to many when they did not falter in the early rounds. In the Elite Eight, the team faced Gene Keady's Purdue Boilermakers, the top seed. Purdue's Glen "Big Dog" Robinson was the nation's leading scorer and soon to be the first player taken in the 1994 NBA Draft. Coach K's troops did a good job of limiting a banged-up Big Dog, but at halftime the game was tied at 32. Krzyzewski was impressed by the play of Duke freshman Jeff Capel and told him he'd be "the guy" in the second half. Grant Hill, by then the team leader, echoed this encouragement.

Grant Hill ignites a fast break during the 1994 NCAA final against Arkansas.

In the second half, Hill picked up his fourth foul and went to the bench. As promised, Capel took charge and finished with nineteen points, seven assists, and four rebounds in a 69–60 win. Hill apologized to his coach for getting in foul trouble, but Krzyzewski told him he won the game at halftime. "You won it when you told Jeff Capel that he could be great today. And he was. In fact, he was the difference in the game when you were out. He lifted everybody else up to a higher level. You won the game for us just as sure as if you had been on the court the entire time."[5]

In the Final Four, Duke dispatched Florida and advanced to yet another NCAA title game. Led by Corliss "Big Nasty" Williamson, their opponents, the Arkansas Razorbacks, played a frenetic brand of full-court defense known as "Forty Minutes of Hell." Duke built a ten-point lead in the second half before Arkansas clawed their way back to a tie. With the game tied at 70, Razorbacks guard Scotty Thurman sank a back-breaking three as the shot clock expired. In the wake of Arkansas' 76–72 victory, Coach K said, "It's a game where somebody won and nobody lost."[6]

Hill a Hall of Famer?

One of the best all-around players of his generation, Grant Hill became eligible for the Hall of Fame in 2017. After becoming the first player in ACC history with more than 1,900 points, 700 rebounds, 400 assists, 200 steals, and 100 blocked shots, he was the third pick in the NBA draft, joining the Detroit Pistons. Hill, along with Jason Kidd of the Dallas Mavericks, was named Rookie of the Year his first year out. His later career included seven All-Star teams (five All-NBA selections) and a gold medal from the 1996 Olympic Games in Atlanta. He also received the NBA Sportsmanship Award three times.

THE SPIRIT WAS WILLING, THE FLESH WEAK

Then, early in the 1994–95 campaign, Mike Krzyzewski hit a

wall. In the course of eleven consecutive NCAA Tournament appearances and seven Final Fours in the last nine years, the demands on him had steadily grown. He was college basketball's most visible, popular, and in-demand coach. "No" was not a word in his vocabulary. He had tried to fulfill every request made to him, whether it was speaking at banquets, serving on committees, or participating in charity events. "All my life I trained to do one thing, and that was coach," he said a few years later. "I never planned on being a celebrity. And when I became one, I had no idea how to handle it."[7]

The demands Coach K faced affected his team, too. Their coach had devoted less time to recruiting and made uncharacteristic mistakes in that department. He admitted to being distracted in meetings with his players. "The truth is that I had violated the basic premises that originally allowed us to achieve all our success,"[8] he said later. What mattered most were the things that had so impressed Grant Hill about Quin Snyder's speech. And if Krzyzewski could get back to helping his student-athletes master the concepts of commitment, toughness, honesty, and integrity, winning games wouldn't be a big problem.

Now, though, his body was telling him to slow down. It began with leg and foot problems, which led to a herniated disc in his back. He lost weight and grew weaker, and the pain became overwhelming. He could barely eat or sleep. "He looked like he was eighty years old,"[9] said Mickie. He had back surgery on the eve of the 1994–95 season.

The last thing Krzyzewski wanted to do was miss a practice, let alone actual games, so he rushed his recovery from surgery and

Nolan Richardson (*center*), coach of the Arkansas Razorbacks, celebrates their triumph over Duke in the 1994 title game. Arkansas fell just short of back-to-back championships, losing to UCLA in the 1995 final.

returned to the court with a back brace. After suffering a setback, he was hospitalized in January 1995. He tried desperately to complete two weeks of physical therapy and return to the bench. More agonizing than the physical pain was having to watch his team struggle without him. Though their record was 9–3 when he went out, Duke went 4–15 in the nineteen games played without Coach K.

It was obvious to Mickie and Coach K's doctors, friends, and associates that two weeks wasn't going to do it. He finally accepted the fact that he was out for the year. "The truth is that I felt relieved," Coach K said later. "I was blinded by my emotions and my commitment not to miss work." Athletic director Tom Butters told him,

"Mike, this is your job whenever you're ready to come back … I don't want anyone else as my basketball coach."[10]

Coach K came to see the time away as a turning point in his life, and the adversity only made him a better, stronger person. When he returned, Krzyzewski had more help screening requests to keep his commitments manageable, and he resolved to strike a truer balance between all the people and things in his life. "I don't want to be one-dimensional and have my whole life revolve around a series of screens and picks to produce a basket," he said. "It's funny, but out of the dark days of that season came light and renewal. It was good to know that I was mortal."[11]

Without a stellar recruiting class in the fold, Duke did not begin the 1995–96 season as favorites. The team opened conference play at 0–4. Before he knew it, Coach K was looking at a 4–7 record in the ultra-competitive ACC and knew they'd have to be no worse than 8–8 to earn an invite to the Big Dance. The team captain that season was senior Chris Collins,

Conference of Champions

Founded in 1953, the Atlantic Coast Conference (ACC) was the first league to hold its own postseason tournament (today, most do). Half of the original eight schools are located in the "Tobacco Road" region of North Carolina—Duke, UNC-Chapel Hill (better known as North Carolina), North Carolina State, and Wake Forest—and these schools have historically dominated the conference. The ACC has produced more than a dozen national champions, with North Carolina and Duke leading the way. In 2017 the conference sent nine of its fifteen teams to the NCAA Tournament—only the 2011 Big East had more entries in the bracket (eleven).

and Krzyzewski had a feeling they'd go as far as Collins could take them. Collins was the kind of player who got even more excited when a teammate made a great play than he did after one of his own. He'd taken over a hard-fought road game against NC State in January, capping off his effort with a game-winning three-pointer to register Duke's first conference win of the season.

Coach K called his captain aside and told Collins that for the rest of the season he should play instinctively and aggressively, with no fear of failure. "Now, I'm not going to mention this to the rest of the team," said Krzyzewski. "Anything you do, Chris, will be okay—and I'll cover your back. But from here on out we win or lose with you."[12]

It was the right offer for the right player at the right time. Collins averaged twenty-three points per game over the next five games, and Duke won them all. In the last game of the regular season, Collins scored eighteen points in twenty-five minutes of play before injuring his foot. The Blue Devils lost, but they'd gotten to 8–8 in the conference and could take part in March Madness.

> ***"Coach K will always tell you the truth."***[13]
> **—Steve Wojciechowski**

Making it back to the tournament wasn't as important as Collins' impact on the next generation. "Chris Collins' undying enthusiasm set the program back on the right path,"[14] said Coach K. Understudies Steve "Wojo" Wojciechowski and Trajan Langdon learned from his example. To this day, the Duke program relies on players to pass down coaches' lessons and standards of excellence to the next generation.

Though a passionate player, "Wojo" had some athletic limitations that relegated him to backup duty his first two years. He always played hard and inspired teammates to do the same. After the Blue Devils lost in the first round, the guard lost weight over the summer and came back noticeably quicker. Langdon, the first prominent Division I player from Alaska, was more physically talented, and his long-range shooting prowess earned him the nickname "the Alaskan Assassin." Their competition came to the point that Coach K knew he'd have to start both of them. Krzyzewski has never put a high premium on positions and plays his best combination regardless of their labels, or even their size.

Though the 1996–97 team lost to Providence in the second round of the NCAAs, they had surpassed expectations. No one would have picked them to win the ACC regular season title that year, which they did. Duke was regaining its lost stature. "You guys helped make me love coaching again," Coach K told his team. "I wasn't sure after last year if that could happen ... Don't feel sad because we lost. Only one team in this thing isn't going to lose. Feel sad because the journey's over."[15]

6

DEVILISHLY CLEVER

In 1997, Coach K produced his most heralded freshman class in years. He'd gone back to his old recruiting method of hand-picking prospects with the right combination of academic and athletic potential, then spending as much time getting to know them as NCAA rules allowed. This ensured that program and player were a fit.

Aided by dynamic freshmen Elton Brand and Shane Battier, the Blue Devils played their way into the final eight. After adding Corey Maggette in 1998–99, another instant contributor, the Blue Devils became one of the most dangerous teams in the nation. They entered the tournament as a number-one seed, with a single loss on their record. Wojo was gone, but senior Trajan Langdon carried his mantle of leadership.

In the Final Four, Krzyzewski's bunch beat a Michigan State team that would be national champions the following year. Now Duke squared off against the UConn Huskies for all the marbles. While the Blue Devils were heavily favored to win their first national title since 1992, UConn had only one more loss on the year and were ranked number one much of the way. They also had Richard "Rip" Hamilton, who would become a three-time All-Star and win an NBA title with the Detroit Pistons.

> ***"You never want to let a mistake be the last time an individual dares to try."*** [1]
>
> **—Coach K**

Coach K was heading for hip replacement surgery and could barely stand during the game. He believes it hindered his team. "They got behind and started to feel sorry for themselves, and I couldn't grab them emotionally and say, 'Stop it!' They needed a coach who could bring the intensity you should bring to a championship game, and I didn't have it." [2] Perhaps it wasn't Duke's day, but every time UConn scored, Langdon answered. Continuing the team's line of leaders at the point guard position, he refused to let his team lose and made one superb play after another. With 1:42 left in the game, he drilled a three-pointer to trim UConn's lead to one.

In the final minute of the game, Coach K relied on Langdon again. But heavy defensive pressure led to his star being called for traveling. Then, after two UConn free throws, Langdon turned the ball over trying to uncork a desperate three-pointer. "The ball was in our best player's hands with an opportunity to win the game," said Krzyzewski. "And that's the way it should be. They played good defense—that's it." [3]

He'd followed his heart, and he could live with the result. Krzyzewski was certain Duke would have lost by double digits without the Alaskan Assassin. It was a disappointing end to Langdon's college career, but a reminder that you can't win every game. "I'll win or lose with Trajan Langdon," Coach K reiterated after the game. "I'll walk down any road with Trajan Langdon … I have a hard time being sad. I don't coach for winning, I coach for relationships. I got the best."[4]

In Coach K's eyes, it was still a great year. "Every time we've made the Final Four has been a thrill … When we didn't go for four straight seasons, it made getting back in 1999 that much sweeter."[5] But Krzyzewski's satisfaction was short-lived. He thought Elton Brand might jump to the NBA, but he was shocked when Corey Maggette and William Avery did as well. Another key player transferred to another school. "In twenty-five years of coaching, nothing had ever happened to me like this before—nothing even close."[6] The team that had won thirty-seven games the year before—a record total, at the time—had lost all but three of its significant contributors. If that

Another "Late Bloomer"

Like Mike Krzyzewski, Connecticut coach Jim Calhoun was initially thought of as a coach who "couldn't win the big one." After building Northeastern into an unlikely fixture in the NCAA Tournament, he reached the Sweet Sixteen or Elite Eight in half of his first twelve seasons at UConn and won 270 games, but didn't earn a national championship until the Huskies' 1998–99 win over Duke. Under Calhoun, UConn would win two more NCAA championships. The Hall of Famer retired in 2012 with 873 victories and a reputation as one of the best coaches ever.

A visibly moved Coach K at the trophy ceremony after Duke topped Arizona to win the 2001 national title. The eight seasons since his last trophy had often been marked by pain and uncertainty.

wasn't enough, Coach K was again bedridden, this time as he recuperated from hip replacement surgery. "In many ways, I began to feel down and alone,"[7] he confessed.

The three major returning players—Chris Carrawell, Nate James, and Shane Battier—visited their coach at home to promise they'd be there for him. He was touched that they'd come to lift his spirits. Asked if he was okay, Coach K said, "I am okay now that you guys are here." He told them that despite it all, this year's team would be good. "Do you believe it?" he asked. Carrawell replied, "Coach, if you say it, I believe it."[8]

The visit and this conversation had a huge impact on Krzyzewski. "After a difficult time for me and the Duke program, those three players showed me that they truly cared."[9]

Already considered the best defender in college ball, Battier had an underdeveloped offensive game. Until this point he'd averaged less than ten points per game. Coach K thought it was due more to humility than any limitation of talent. Throughout the offseason, he tried to get Battier into the habit of visualizing himself as a big-time scorer, and the conference's player of the year. "Shane needed to imagine because, by doing so, when the time came and he actually found himself in those situations, he would feel as if he had already been there,"[10] said Krzyzewski.

Though resistant at first, Battier eventually embraced his coach's plan for him. "After awhile, with that kind of encouragement, I started to believe it myself,"[11] said Battier. That season he led the team in scoring and was third in both rebounds and assists.

With Battier, James, and Carrawell as captains, Duke finished 29–5 and were both regular season and tournament champions of the ACC. Though they lost to Florida in the Sweet Sixteen (the Gators would reach the title game), Coach K's squad surpassed all expectations.

ADAPT OR PERISH

In 2000–2001, a Krzyzewski favorite, Chris Collins, joined the coaching staff. Battier and James were again team leaders, and Coach K knew Battier was ready for an even larger role. This time the forward didn't need any convincing. He took his game to the next level, upping his scoring average to almost twenty points per game and winning National Player of the Year honors. Battier's jersey was retired before a February game in which the Blue Devils handed Georgia Tech its most lopsided defeat in almost thirty years.

Center Carlos Boozer was a pivotal player for Duke as their best big body. Late in the season, he went through a rough stretch, and it got back to Coach K that the burly sophomore thought he wasn't getting the ball enough. "Whenever there is a minor thing that might turn into something major, I jump on it immediately," Krzyzewski wrote in his book *Five-Point Play*. "Well, this was one of those things."[12] He believes individual meetings with his players are indispensable, and he arranged one with Boozer. Boozer admitted the rumor was true and Krzyzewski told him, matter-of-factly, what his real problems were. It was a long list, and suddenly the big man was crying. Coach K told him that was the best thing he could have done, because it showed that he cared. In Duke's next game, Boozer was dominant in the paint, collecting a season-high thirteen rebounds and converting a crucial three-point play late in the game.

> ***"Belief raises your confidence level and allows you to try things impossible to do by yourself."***[13]
>
> **—Coach K**

When Boozer was injured late in the year, it looked as though Duke's title aspirations would be dashed. But the setback prompted Coach

K and his staff to figure out a new way forward. They came up with a bold plan to play to the team's strengths. Meeting a disconsolate group of players at 6 a.m., Krzyzewski promised them they would win the national championship if they did everything he asked. Then, at practice, they simulated the new run-and-gun style in the same four-minute increments the game is played in due to TV timeouts. The idea was to exhaust opponents with their improvisational, up-tempo style.

The players were initially skeptical. For the system to work, Krzyzewski needed to start freshman Chris Duhon over his senior captain and rock through hard times, Nate James. He didn't know how James would respond. Of this time, James later said, "I thought, 'hey man, you only have a month to go [before graduation]. Is it going to be a bad month or a good month?' I was thinking about my teammates. That's what got me over feeling sorry for myself."[14]

By the time they played their next game, on the road against North Carolina, everyone had bought in. "After four minutes, we were leading, and the whole place was shocked," remembered Battier. "Even we were a bit shocked. We didn't know it was going to work that well. But we all thought, 'You know what? We've got something here.'"[15]

The final score of the ACC final was Duke 95, North Carolina 85, and no one cheered harder than Boozer. Krzyzewski called this victory one of the most memorable moments of his career. "Instead of letting the loss of Carlos Boozer destroy our morale, we actually used that event as a rallying point," he said. "We became a deeper team—both mentally and physically."[16]

Teams didn't know what to do with Duke's frenetic pace of play. After the blowout over North Carolina to win the ACC and notch Coach K's six hundredth career victory, the Blue Devils went into the NCAA Tournament as the number-one team in the nation. Then, despite Boozer's return, the team came out flat in the Sweet Sixteen. UCLA gave them a scare before Duke came alive in the second half, thanks to some impassioned pleading from Coach K at halftime.

After dispatching USC to make the Final Four, Duke found the Maryland Terrapins and coach Gary Williams more than ready for them. The teams had already played each other three times that season: First, Duke won on the road in a comeback dubbed "The Miracle Minute." Then the Terrapins avenged this defeat by spoiling Duke's Senior Day. Finally the Blue Devils took the "rubber match" in the ACC Tournament.

Maryland came out of the gates 39–17, stunning to silence the Duke fans in attendance. Coach K called timeout and rallied the troops. By halftime Maryland's lead had been slashed to 49–38. During the break, Krzyzewski made two key adjustments: he moved Jason Williams to shooting guard and had Duhon play the point. He also assigned Nate James to cover Maryland star Juan Dixon due to his four-inch height advantage. After lighting up Duke for sixteen in the first half, Dixon mustered one field goal on eight attempts in the second. Getting more shots at two-guard, Williams hit a big three to give Duke their first lead. They pulled away to win by nine, completing the largest comeback in Final Four history.

In the championship game, Duke got out to a 35–33 halftime lead against Lute Olson's Arizona Wildcats, but Krzyzewski didn't like the way things were going. Though he'd used Boozer sparingly since his return, the center started in the second half and played a major role. Mike Dunleavy was battling a shoulder injury and struggled in the Maryland game. Today he'd managed three points in the first half. At the break, Collins and Coach K convinced the forward he was critical to the cause. Inspired, Dunleavy hit a trio of three pointers in forty-six seconds.

In the last ten minutes of the game, the Blue Devils took it to another level, playing in perfect harmony. Every time Arizona tried to pull away, Duke rose to the occasion. Even Jason Williams, who'd been struggling, nailed a three that was the dagger in an 82–72 victory. "I did a double-take," said Williams when Krzyzewski called the play for him. "'Me?' I thought. 'Are you sure you want me? I just made a turnover. I'm not playing well. And you want me to take the shot right now at this crucial point

No Shame in Shane's Game

Shane Battier's distinguished career at Duke led to him being the No. 6 pick in the 2001 NBA Draft. He earned All-Rookie First Team honors as a member of the Memphis Grizzlies before settling into a fourteen-year career as a cerebral defensive specialist. The forward was a key reserve on two championship teams, averaging 11.6 points per game for the Miami Heat in the 2012 NBA Finals, and he hit six three-pointers in the Heat's 2013 Game Seven victory over the San Antonio Spurs. In 2017, Battier became Miami's director of basketball development and analytics.

The Blue Devils acknowledge their fans after winning the championship. The team overcame injury and adversity to reinvent themselves late in the 2000–2001 season. The results were remarkable.

in the game …?' That gave me a tremendous burst of energy, and I thought, 'Okay, I trust Coach, I can do it.'"[17]

Having realized Coach K's vision for him, Shane Battier would graduate as a member of the national champions. "He always possessed the tools necessary to be a star and a great leader, and he was always incredibly talented and smart, but Shane only fully realized his potential when he allowed himself to imagine great things," said Krzyzewski. "As a result, his teammates and I were able to go along for the ride as all of Shane Battier's dreams came true."[18]

7

COULD THE COUNTRY STILL COMPETE?

Coach K has been a contributor to the US national team since 1979, when he was an assistant coach under Bob Knight at the Pan-American Games. They teamed up again to coach the last amateur-only team to capture the gold for the United States at the 1984 Summer Olympics in Los Angeles. Coach K also assisted Chuck Daly with 1992's gold medal winners in Atlanta. The first US squad to feature active NBA players, 1992's lineup was known as the "Dream Team," and its roster was loaded with the greatest stars of the era. Coach K got to observe the habits of legends such as Michael Jordan, Magic Johnson, Larry Bird, Charles Barkley, and the unique Utah

Jazz combo of Karl Malone and John Stockton. Duke's Christian Laettner was the only college player named to the team.

After that, the gap between the Americans' talent and the world's narrowed quickly. The United States soon learned that a collection of superstars could no longer waltz in and win gold medals. At the Athens Games in 2004, the Americans lost to Argentina and went home with the bronze, largely because, in Krzyzewski's eyes, they didn't have enough time to establish the right standards,

Coach K accepted the challenge of restoring the US Olympic team's dominance. Anything less than gold medals at the 2008 Beijing Olympics would be seen as abject failure.

camaraderie, and chemistry. That team was assembled just four months before Olympic competition.

Krzyzewski and Jerry Colangelo, managing director of USA Basketball, agreed that on any given night the NBA All-Stars could be beaten by a more cohesive group. If the United States was going to win gold at the 2008 Summer Olympics in Beijing, their national team would need time to develop as a unit. Colangelo asked Coach K to lead them on that three-year journey.

Weighing whether or not to accept the offer, Coach K had a sometimes-contentious discussion with his family. His wife and daughters were concerned that he would be overworked and exhausted. "But I explained how I feel about challenges, how they keep me fresh, young and hungry,"[1] said Krzyzewski. Ultimately his family gave him their unconditional support, and he became the coach of the United States national team.

In this situation, there could be no moral victory in defeat. Krzyzewski was building a team to

A Nightmare for Opposing Teams

Dubbed the "Dream Team," the 1992 US Olympic basketball team was the talk of the town at the Barcelona Games. Ten of the twelve players on the roster were included on a 1996 list of the fifty greatest players in the history of the NBA. Their margin of victory was 43.8 points per game. The rest of the world took this as a challenge, and kids around the globe were inspired to pick up a basketball. International players became fixtures in the first round of the NBA Draft and, before long, the United States had to adapt or settle for second place—at best.

take back the title of best in the world. The only way to do that was to come back from Beijing with gold medals hanging around their necks.

Krzyzewski's pitch to players was that they could regain the respect of the international community and reestablish the United States as the gold standard for basketball. Coach K didn't shy away from players who'd lost in 2004, either. "In some ways, these guys had more at stake than the others, and they were able to help their teammates comprehend the greater context of what we were trying to accomplish,"[3] he said.

> ***"The greatest pride comes from being part of something you could never do alone—being part of a team."[2]***
>
> **—Coach K**

Though the team rotated thirty-three players on and off its active roster, Coach K wanted to bring to China twelve men who knew the international game and played with a similar level of cohesion as their competitors. Fortunately, it wasn't difficult to find a constellation of stars willing to make the three-year commitment. The final twelve included past-and-future NBA champions Kobe Bryant, Dwyane Wade, and LeBron James, but every member of that team was a franchise player in his own right.

The team had to play a series of tournaments before Beijing, with the first coming less than a year after Coach K was hired. At the FIBA World Championship in Japan, the United States lost to Greece in the semifinals. "I have never suffered a more devastating loss in my career as a head basketball coach,"[4] said Coach K. Once the pain subsided, he let the loss become a learning experience. The team hadn't yet learned enough about the international style of play, and the roster wasn't quite right yet. For an injection of experience, Krzyzewski brought on the Duke killer Jason Kidd. Now in the latter stages of an illustrious NBA career, Kidd would become another coach on the floor and a team leader alongside Bryant and James.

Once the team was assembled, the goal was getting to know each other and the international game. As James put it, to be a team you have to be a family first. They convened in a meeting room before every practice. Coach K did this to foster face-to-face communication as a group. At one point he shared something he told his college players. "When we talk to each other, we look each other in the eye, we tell each other the truth, and we treat each other like men."[5] He described how important it was to him that they always have honest and respectful communication, because it would develop the trust that was so essential to teamwork.

At one point, Krzyzewski brought in Colonel Bob Brown, whom he'd coached at West Point, and soldiers who had suffered serious injuries in combat to address the team. "There is clearly no comparison between taking a charge in a basketball game and putting your life on the line in a combat situation," said Coach K. "But what I hoped our team could tap into is that we *do* have something in common with the soldiers—[the people] who we represent."[6] The selflessness embodied by these wounded warriors gave Coach K's players a greater appreciation for their own mission: to make their country proud.

At the 2007 Americas Championship, Bob Knight visited the team. In a moment alone, he emphasized that Krzyzewski was as good at his job as his players were at theirs. "As a college coach, I like to think that I help boys become men," said Coach K. "But I did sometimes question what I had to offer this group, who were already men and had found much success in the NBA. Coach Knight knew that I had accepted the biggest challenge of my career. A challenge of this magnitude can bring about fear, and that fear can change you. My coach wanted to ensure that would not happen to me."[7]

As the 2008 Summer Olympics drew nearer, Coach K and his players locked down the team's style of play and collective identity. That identity, as it was with any given Blue Devils group, would be based on defense. Kobe Bryant was on board. "No matter where you play—if you're playing here, if you're playing on Mars—if you can shut somebody down and rebound the basketball, you're going to win …"[8] The players agreed that they would not employ the showy, offense-first style other national teams might expect from NBA All-Stars. They would do the dirty work necessary to win.

In fact, Bryant toned down his prolific scoring to focus on being a defensive stopper. It reminded the team that defense was their shared focus. But his competitive nature also stood out. "He is incredibly unique because he is that rare breed of person who lives for the crucial moment," said Coach K. "People like Kobe find the ultimate high

Coach K needed NBA superstars like Dwyane Wade to embrace the same principles of teamwork he'd been teaching college kids for years, such as forthright communication.

in the big game, the big moment, crunch time. When others would be shaking, he smiles. When others would be hesitating, he can't wait."[9]

NO MORAL VICTORIES IN BEIJING

After a poor showing against Australia in the team's final exhibition game, Coach K had a sleepless night. Were they truly ready for the well-oiled machines they'd face at the Olympics? Krzyzewski studied the game-tape and had heated discussions with his staff about what to do. He also met with Kidd and Bryant to walk through what they needed to improve personally. Finally, he addressed the whole team about being accountable to the standards of excellence they'd all agreed upon. His team felt galvanized by the message. In that moment Coach K proved he could coach NBA superstars.

The six members of the team who lost to Greece in 2006 were eager for a rematch in Beijing, three games into pool play. The United States won 92–69. "We played like we had something to prove," said Coach K."[10] His attention to defense translated in China. The United States led the Olympic field in opponents' field goal percentage, steals, blocks, forced turnovers, and points off turnovers.

Team USA entered the medal round undefeated. From here on out it was like the NCAA Tournament—win or go home. Their first opponent was Australia. Not only had the Aussies played well the first time around, they had the kind of shooting that gave any team a chance in a one-game situation. The Americans came out tight and clung to a one-point advantage at the end of the first quarter. After halftime tweaks, the United States came out of the locker room hot and made a 14–0 run, ultimately outdistancing their opponents 116–85. The team had cured what ailed them in their last meeting with Australia.

> *"Preparation is key if you hope to operate well under pressure."*[11]
>
> —Coach K

In the next round, Coach K had his guys so prepared for Argentina's explosive Manu Ginobli that it actually threw them off their game when he was injured in the first ten minutes of the semi-final game. The Australians, as defending Olympic champions, still had indomitable spirit and another NBA player, Luis Scola, on their side. Still, once the US team adjusted their game plan, they came together and got the win.

The gold medal game was at hand. Three years of preparation had boiled down to forty minutes of basketball. Would all their hard work be for naught? It didn't look good when Bryant and James hit the bench early with two fouls apiece. This threw off the substitution pattern the players expected and forced Dwyane Wade and Deron Williams to pick up the slack, especially with the United States trailing 13–9. But they made it work. Within forty-five seconds, Wade had reeled off a lay-up and converted a three-point play.

It seemed as though the United States might pull away until Spain's stars Pau Gasol, Rudy Fernandez, and Ricky Rubio—all three NBA talents with varying degrees of pro experience at that time—fought back from a fourteen-point lead to make the score 69–61 at halftime. Until this point the United States had held teams to an average score of 75 per game, so Spain's offense

Another Chance to Make His Nation Proud

At the 2012 Olympic Games in London, Mike Krzyzewski returned to coach USA Basketball to a gold medal. Five players returned from the 2008 team, while newcomers included Kevin Durant, Russell Westbrook, and James Harden. Though they lacked the size of their predecessors, this group played to their strengths with a small, quick lineup that excelled in outside shooting. The Americans trailed in the fourth quarter just once en route to an 8–0 record. The finals pitted the Americans against Spain once again, with the United States coming out on top 107–100.

Coach K and his team completed their mission in Beijing and made their fellow Americans proud of Team USA. Coach K returned to lead the United States to gold medals at the 2012 and 2016 Olympic Games.

was on fire. Given their foul trouble, Bryant and James weren't playing defense with their usual reckless abandon.

In the third quarter, Carmelo Anthony came up big to stake Coach K's team to an eleven-point lead. But Juan Carlos Navarro made a series of big plays for Spain to keep them in the game. The United States entered the final period up 91–82. Then Gasol and Fernandez ripped off seven straight points to narrow that lead to two. Krzyzewski called timeout. It was Kobe Bryant time. The "Black Mamba" went to work, culminating in a rare four-point play when he hit a three, was fouled, and sank the free throw. Though this fouled out Fernandez, Spain still answered with a three and remained in striking distance with about two minutes left. That's when Dwyane Wade slammed the door, hitting a three of his own to push the lead back to seven.

With the 118–107 win, Coach K's men had earned the nickname "Redeem Team." He was used to helping boys become men, but on this occasion men became boys. The NBA superstars showed a child-like joy at this happy end to their journey. On the medal stand, they stood arm in arm. Posing for pictures, they put all twelve of their gold medals around Krzyzewski's neck (Olympic coaches do not receive medals of their own). And they honored their opponents, who had proven more than worthy of Olympic glory themselves. "There is no doubt in my mind that we could have lost both those games had we not together formed relationships, established standards, and engaged in some honest self-assessment," said Coach K. "No matter how talented the personnel we put on the floor, we can no longer succeed without embracing the notion of team."[12]

8

A COACH WHO REALLY CARES

Since his program's rise to prominence, Mike Krzyzewski has taken the opportunity to parley that visibility into benefits for the community. In 2012, Krzyzewski's impact was honored with the US Basketball Writers Association's Wayman Tisdale Humanitarian Award. "Usually whatever I have given, I get back more,"[1] said Coach K, who is especially passionate about programs for children and students. He chairs the board of directors and leads fundraising efforts for the Emily Krzyzewski Center, named for his mom, who passed away in 1996 at the age of eighty-four. Founded in 2006, the center helps academically focused but low-income K–12 students and graduates navigate the path to college. "I am so proud that the center was named in honor of my late mother, whose hard work and commitment to family provided me and my brother with opportunities to imagine,"[2] said the Duke legend.

Duke's student fans do not lack for enthusiasm. The "Cameron Crazies" make their arena inhospitable to opposing teams, while giving the Blue Devils unconditional support.

Mike and his wife, Mickie Krzyzewski, chaired the national advisory board for the Duke Children's Hospital and have been active supporters of the Children's Miracle Network for many years. The couple and their daughters, Debbie, Lindy, and Jamie, also teamed up on stay-in-school programs and awareness campaigns dealing with alcohol, drug abuse, and drunk driving. More informally, Coach K has been known to brighten the day of many a sick child. "Whenever our team is feeling a little bit blue about a loss, I'll take some of the players over to the Duke Medical Center to visit with the kids," he said. "Right away, we get our perspective back."[3]

Cancer claimed the lives of both Mike's parents and, in 2013, that of his brother William too. Unsurprisingly, Coach K has backed efforts to combat the disease. "I do a lot of work for the Cancer Comprehensive Center, Coaches vs. Cancer, and I'm on the board of directors for the Jimmy V Foundation,"[4] he wrote in *Coaching from the Heart.*

To expand his teaching opportunities beyond the umbrella of his team, Coach K has co-written several inspirational books that impart the life lessons he has learned. Listed in the "Further Reading" section, these titles are notable because there is no traditional autobiography for Coach K, or even an authorized biography; he tells personal stories purely to share with others the universal value of his experiences.

While coaching US national teams and doing charity work would be enough to keep anyone busy, Krzyzewski's main job is, of course, coaching the men's basketball team at Duke. Still, his emphasis on education begins there, where academic standards are rigorous, both in admissions and graduation requirements.

They Go Batty for the Blue Devils

When Duke's student fans chant "our house!" at Cameron Indoor Stadium, they really mean it. Coach K considers the "Cameron Crazies" as much a part of the team as the players. They act as a "sixth man" during home games, making lots of noise to support Duke and rattle their opponents. Tickets are so hard to come by that students camp out for weeks, rotating in and out of tents to save their spots. On many occasions Coach K has paid visits to this tent city, known as "Krzyzewskiville," bringing fans pizza or inviting them to a pregame strategy session.

Coach K has often told the parents of recruits that their son would have every chance to make it to the NBA if he was good enough and, if not, he'd leave with a prestigious Duke degree. The coaching staff teaches players time management strategies and monitors their academic progress. "Basketball players are not going to simply scrape by in their studies at Duke University," said Krzyzewski. "I expect every player we recruit to graduate. And I tell them so right up front."[5]

In fact, Coach K has famously refused to hang a team's banner in Cameron Indoor Stadium until every member of the team has graduated. The 1990 team's Final Four banner waited nine years to reach the rafters. Despite the trend of top players jumping to the NBA after one year, Duke's 2017 graduation success rate was 100 percent, meaning that each of Krzyzewski's players who should have earned a degree between 2013 and 2016 did so.

> ***"Giving back breeds giving back. It is simply the right thing to do."[6]***
>
> **—Coach K**

Coach K holds his student-athletes to a high standard. He has never given out every possible scholarship he could have. "When my staff and I decide which kids to recruit, we don't merely look at the youngster's athletic ability, statistics, and grades, we look at how they treat their parents, how they interact with their classmates, and what other ways they contribute to their communities,"[7] said Coach K.

His relationship with his players remains very personal. "Several times a year, my wife Mickie and I have the team over to the house,"

Coach K encourages forward Kyle Singler, MVP of Duke's 2010 championship squad. Krzyzewski is a master of balancing honest critique and unwavering faith in his players' capabilities.

said Krzyzewski. "We will serve a casual meal, put football games on the television, and allow the guys to relax and be themselves. I often meet with players one-on-one and ask them questions about their lives: their families, their girlfriends, their classes. These are all opportunities to show my team that they are not merely basketball players to me. I genuinely care for each and every one of them, and after our time together at Duke, I continue to care about them. I absolutely love when my former players call me to ask for my input or advice, or even just to catch up."[8]

This tradition reflects Coach K's desire to ensure that everyone on his team feels comfortable expressing themselves. He once gave a long speech he considered the basketball equivalent of the Gettysburg Address, but it slowly became clear the underlying message hadn't resonated. A few minutes later he asked the players if they'd understood it, and Shane Battier admitted that they hadn't. In thirty seconds, a chastened Krzyzewski conveyed the intent of his fifteen-minute speech and told Battier that if it happened again, he needed to know.

After Battier and company's 2001 win over Arizona, only two coaches had more national titles than Krzyzewski's trio of trophies: Adolph Rupp (four) and the legendary John Wooden (ten). The low point of 1995 was long behind him. One of the proudest days of Coach K's life was his enshrinement in the Naismith Basketball Hall of Fame, also in 2001. At one time, Mike's father shortened the family's distinctive Polish name to "Kross," hoping it would help him find employment. Mike knew his father would feel great pride at "Krzyzewski" being listed among the greatest names in basketball history. "To think that at one point my dad had to change his name, and now—his real name, our family name, the name we are all proud of—would be looked upon with honor and distinction,"[9] marveled the happy coach.

Before coaching Kobe Bryant at the 2008 Olympics, Krzyzewski missed two chances at it. Bryant has said he would have attended Duke had he not decided to go straight from high school to the NBA in 1996. Then, in 2004, Bryant's Los Angeles Lakers offered Coach K a $40 million contract to jump ship. Krzyzewski called his former athletic director, Tom Butters, for advice and was told to follow his heart. Coach K knew where his heart was. He wanted to show Duke the same commitment Butters had, after the rocky start to his career. But equally important is what drives him to coach for a living. "I realized I'm not just a basketball coach," he said of an earlier flirtation with the Boston Celtics. "And if I were in the NBA, that's what I'd be. I want to be a teacher and work with kids and see them grow up. What's neat is that I can win a lot of basketball games while I'm doing that."[10]

WOULD "ONE-AND-DONES" BE HIS UNDOING?

One of the reasons a coach old-fashioned enough to use the word "neat" might leave Duke was the "one-and-done," a term coined in 2007, when the NBA changed its rules to require that a player be at least one year out of high school before he was eligible for the NBA Draft. Consequently, stars who would have bypassed college entirely, the way Bryant and James did in years past, now had to spend one year on campus (or play overseas). It simply wasn't enough time to teach them the way Coach K would like, and not nearly enough time to see his pupils mature. And more and more players were foregoing their college eligibility to turn pro.

The early exits were certainly not limited to Duke's program, but they continued to sap Krzyzewski's team of the depth, chemistry, and experience he strived to create. After promising underclassmen defected to the draft, Duke's 2004–2005 team wasn't even ranked in the national top ten entering the season. Despite these hurdles, J. J. Redick was an emerging talent, Shelden Williams was a force inside, and the incoming freshmen contributed to a season that saw Duke finish 25–5, win the ACC Tournament, and begin as the number one seed on the NCAA bracket. All looked promising for the Blue Devils, but in the Sweet Sixteen that year they were ousted by Michigan State.

By the next year, Krzyzewski had doubts about continuing his coaching career at all, let alone staying at Duke. His childhood friend Dennis "Moe" Mlynski had weighed in on it. "After our season-ending loss to Louisiana State University in the Sweet Sixteen, Moe came to my hotel room along with my family," Coach K remembered in *Beyond Basketball*. "Long after everyone else had gone to bed, Moe, my wife Mickie and I were still talking. At the end of every season I struggle with what I could have done differently, how I could have done better, and I reevaluate where I am in my life and in my career. Feeling as down as I could be, I found myself wondering if coaching was still what I wanted to be doing … 'Mick,' Moe said to me, and even just hearing the name from my youth brought me back to earth. 'You have always loved to lead.' He put it so simply that I couldn't help but realize he was right."[11]

In 2009–2010, Duke posted an impressive 30–6 record before

After helping Duke reach the 2004 Final Four in his freshman year, Luol Deng (#2) turned pro after playing only one year of college ball.

falling short in the Sweet Sixteen. Coach K had to watch the rival Tar Heels win their second national title in five years, both with the formidable Roy Williams at the helm.

After missing out on five Final Fours in a row, Coach K knew he had to adapt to the new landscape if Duke was going to get back there. With this in mind, in 2009 he recruited Kyrie Irving, a point guard certain to play one year and then make millions as a pro. Irving would join the team in 2010–2011, but there was still a season to play out. Duke began the 2009–2010 campaign with an experienced starting five but no stars to speak of. What they did well was play suffocating defense, and the insertion of seven-footer Brian Zoubek into the starting lineup took their D to another level.

This team displayed another hallmark of a Coach K squad: short memories. "The most important play of the game or life moment on which you should always focus is the next one," said

Instant Offense

Though he never won a national championship in Durham, J. J. Redick was beloved by the Cameron Crazies and reviled by rival fans. The kind of player who could seemingly score at will, he set several records and became Duke's all-time leader in total points, eclipsing Johnny Dawkins' twenty-year-old mark. After winning several national Player of the Year awards in 2006, Redick was taken eleventh overall by the NBA's Orlando Magic. He has been a prolific scorer in spurts and averaged almost sixteen points per game in four years with the Los Angeles Clippers before getting off to an even hotter start with the 76ers in 2017–2018. Redick's was one of thirteen Duke jerseys to be retired in the Blue Devils' basketball history.

Coach K. "It is not about the turnover I committed last time down the court, it's not even about the three-pointer I hit to tie the game, it's about what's next."[12] By instilling this in his teams, Coach K helps them stay in the moment and avoid distraction.

The Blue Devils won the 2010 ACC Tournament, but not in flashy fashion. They were assigned to the South Regional in Houston, home of Duke's Elite Eight opponent, the Baylor Bears. Getting past them was no picnic, but Duke prevailed, 78–71, and made their return to the national semifinals. There, West Virginia was no match for the highly disciplined Blue Devils. Coach K's team would be competing for another NCAA crown.

After outlasting Butler in a hard-fought title game, the 2010 national champions enjoy the CBS presentation of "One Shining Moment," a montage of tournament highlights set to music.

The other finalist, Butler, was a classic Cinderella team. Again the game would be played in hostile territory. The Butler campus was about six miles from Lucas Oil Stadium, site of the Final Four. The Bulldogs were playing defense every bit as ferocious as Duke's. They'd held all five of their tournament foes to fifty-nine or fewer points.

Once the game was underway, neither team could get in any kind of offensive rhythm. Every pass was contested, every shooter found a hand in his face, and every path to the hoop was blocked. The biggest lead of the night, for either team, was a scant five points. Down 60–59, Butler had the ball and thirty-three seconds to play.

> ***"The basic formula of teaching [is] you hear, you forget; you see, you remember; you do, you understand."*** [13]
>
> **—Coach K**

Gordon Hayward rose to launch a potential game-winner, but Zoubek managed to get there in time to challenge the shot, altering his release. Then, showing quickness few knew he had, the center turned and hauled in the rebound. He was fouled with 3.6 seconds left. After making the first one, Zoubek missed the second intentionally. Coach K figured that Butler would get a better shot off the inbounds pass—as Duke did versus Kentucky, in 1992—than they would off a rebound.

Hayward collected the carom and dashed upcourt. His forty-five footer was on target but hit glass, causing the ball to rim out. It would have been a miracle shot and an even-more amazing finish, but time expired and the national championship went to the team from Tobacco Road.

9

COACH K IS ONE OF A KIND

For Coach K, the fist is not a sign of aggression; it is a symbol of togetherness. As he tells his guys, "A basketball team is like the five fingers on your hand. If you can get them all together, you have a fist. That's how I want you to play."[1] If the five players on the court act as one, their play can achieve a perfect symmetry that no handful of individuals could match. "When two equally talented teams are matched up against each other, most often the team that works harder and works together will be victorious,"[2] said Krzyzewski.

Krzyzewski's 2010 national champions certainly embraced the concept of the fist, but the next four seasons were trying. When Kyrie Irving arrived, he injured his toe in December and missed most of the year. He returned for the 2011 NCAA Tournament with only eight games under his belt, and the team chemistry was off. Irving's time with Duke ended in the Sweet Sixteen, along with the Blue Devils' season. To make matters worse, the next year Lehigh gave Duke the boot in the first round of the tourney.

In 2013, Duke reached the Elite Eight but could push no farther. The next year, Coach K brought highly touted recruit Jabari Parker into the fold, but the freshman faltered in the first round of the tournament as the superior experience of Mercer's senior-heavy lineup decided the game.

It was a frustrating time for Krzyzewski, but things turned around in 2014–2015. He notched the thousandth win of his career in February 2015, defeating St. John's at Madison Square Garden. By this time, Coach K had three "one-and-done's" in his starting lineup. "I hate it," he said of the phenomenon. "My thing has always been about developing relationships with the guys I coach. You can't do that in one year. But if I don't have these guys playing for me for a year, then I'll almost certainly have them playing against me for a year."[3]

He Gave Duke One Great Year

In seventh grade, Jahlil Okafor matched his father's height, six-feet-five (196 centimeters), and he grew to almost seven feet (213 cm) tall. Colleges began coveting Okafor before he reached high school. In high school, he won a city championship, several national Player of the Year awards, and gold medals at the FIBA Under-17 and Under-19 World Championships. The five-star recruit was courted by all the top schools but followed Chicago's last prep superstar, Jabari Parker, to Duke. As a Blue Devil, he was the first freshman to win ACC Player of the Year. After winning the 2015 national title, Okafor entered the NBA Draft and was taken third overall by the Philadelphia 76ers.

Despite Krzyzewski's feelings about the rule and its impact on the game, he'd adapted his coaching style to make the most of these "rental" players. "I had to coach them the way I coached the guys who stayed for years," he said. "I had to be demanding from day one—not coddle them, not worry about whether they were going to stay or go, or that they were 'just' freshmen … There's no such thing as a 'young' team anymore. Your team is your team. Period."[4]

This incarnation of Coach K's squad lacked the locked-in defensive mindset of most, because there simply wasn't time for freshmen to master his man-to-man scheme. So he instituted a zone defense that was easier for his young charges to execute. The team went 15–2 after that, including a huge win over undefeated and second-ranked Virginia. "We just kept making plays and shots down the stretch," Krzyzewski said about the vital victory. "That was something we hadn't done the year before—closed against a good team. That told me something about this group."[5]

With a 29–4 record, Duke secured a top seed in the tournament. Coach K's charges dispatched Robert Morris and San Diego State by twenty-nine and nineteen points, respectively, to

With his unstoppable post game, Jahlil Okafor helped Duke secure another national title in 2015.

breeze through to the round of sixteen. There, Justise Winslow made several key plays to edge Utah, and then Duke turned a 51–50 lead into a 66–52 win over the eternally tenacious Gonzaga Bulldogs.

With his twelfth appearance in the Final Four, Coach K matched John Wooden's previously unassailable record. Michigan State broke out to a 14–6 lead before Duke stomped on the gas and sped into half-time up 36–25. After emerging from the locker room on a 6–0 run, that was that. With the 81–61 win, the Blue Devils were bound for yet-another title game.

> ***"As long as I'm healthy and enjoying it, I'll coach. Right now, I'm both."[6]***
>
> **—Coach K**

On the other side of the bracket, Wisconsin had pulled off a massive upset, handing Kentucky their first loss of the season. The Badgers were battle-hardened and well-coached by Bo Ryan. Against Duke, they took command early and did not let up. With 13:23 left in the game, Coach K called timeout. His team was down 48–39 and the outlook was bleak.

Searching for answers, Krzyzewski decided to insert freshman Grayson Allen. A sparkplug who usually gave starters rest in the first half of games, Allen's points-per-game average that year was a meager 4.4. He immediately buried a three to cut Wisconsin's lead to six. Soon thereafter he was fouled in the act of scoring and converted the three-point play to make the score 48–45. The pendulum had swung.

Allen sparked a 27–8 Duke run that culminated when Tyus Jones hit one from downtown to beat the shot clock and give Duke a 66–58 lead. In the end, the final score was 68–63, and the NCAA championship belonged to Duke. "What Grayson did was beyond amazing," declared Coach K. "We've had great players make great plays for us in the past, but the way he came into that game and picked us up was … I can't describe it. We were dead in the water and he saved us."[7]

After that, Jones, Winslow, and Jahlil Okafor declared for the 2015 draft. Coach K brought in Brandon Ingram, who helped Duke reach the Sweet Sixteen before the Lakers selected him second overall. A team loaded with underclassmen lost in the second round of the 2016 NCAA Tournament. As was becoming the norm in Durham, four of them

Another year, another viewing of "One Shining Moment." Here, Coach K and company bask in the joy of their 2015 win over Wisconsin in the NCAA final.

were NBA first-round draft picks. Coach K immediately ushered in a new class topped by four consensus five-star recruits. Senior Grayson Allen was named the team's sole captain. Duke entered the 2017–2018 season ranked number one in several polls, but only made it as far as the Elite 8 in the NCAA tournament.

HE'LL MISS TEACHING MOST OF ALL

Another phase of Coach K's career had reached its apex. After leading the United States to a third consecutive Olympic gold medal at the 2016 Summer Games in Rio de Janeiro, Krzyzewski stepped down as coach of the national team. His decade-long journey concluded with a 24–0 record in the Olympics (88–1 overall). Small forward Carmelo Anthony won gold with all of the Olympic teams in Beijing, London, and Rio. "In 2006, we really started to have a culture," he said. "To be alongside Coach K, he sacrificed so much of his time, his family, coming from the collegiate level, instilling his trust into NBA players and being the face of USA Basketball. I just want to say thanks, and I appreciate that."[8]

Though Coach K may have another title or two in him, he turned seventy-one in February 2018. There is as much speculation about who will succeed him at Duke as there is about the next season's recruiting class. In eight months spanning 2016 and 2017, he had five surgeries to address persistent back and knee

> *"With accomplishment comes confidence and with confidence comes belief. It has to be in that order."*[9]
>
> **—Coach K**

troubles. If Krzyzewski's body continues to betray him, how long can he keep going? But the coach still has that fire in the belly, and he has achieved a healthier balance in his life. "Perhaps the most difficult thing he's had to do in the last twenty-five years is learn how to say no to people because if he didn't, he would never have a chance to sleep,"[10] wrote John Feinstein in his book *The Legends Club.*

Hoisting banners sure is nice, but Coach K's primary motivation has never been glory. "That's not the thing I want more than anything else," he said. "I'd have to have my head examined to think that's the one thing I want more than anything else … I start getting philosophical. I want good family, good health. I want consistent performance and I want the truth much more than I want a national championship."[11]

For Coach K, the hardest thing about his inevitable retirement will be letting go of this powerful teaching tool. "Coaching basketball is my vehicle for life itself—for the larger journey," said Krzyzewski. "If the only reason I coached was to win college

A Bright New Star

In November 2017, Marvin Bagley III became the first Duke player in history to score more than thirty points and grab fifteen-plus rebounds in consecutive games. Amazingly, the six-foot-eleven (211-cm) power forward did it at the tender age of eighteen. The Duke freshman has a breathtaking combination of skills that will only continue to blossom in the NBA. A five-star recruit who averaged twenty-five points per game and ten rebounds in high school, Bagley immediately impressed Coach K. "He still has a lot to learn but he's a hard worker, great listener, great teammate, it's not about him, he wants to win," Krzyzewski said.[12]

In 2017, Marvin Bagley III became the next great talent to don a Duke uniform, if only for a short time.

basketball games, my life would be pretty shallow. I coach not only because I love it, but because I have the chance to teach and interact with young people."[13] On another occasion, Duke's commander said, "I'm no different than the professor in the engineering school. I want my young people to be successes."[14]

When he does walk away, Krzyzewski will be grateful for the game's return on his investment in it. "I love the game and it's been great to me," said the coach. "I hate when people say the game owes them something. We owe the game."[15] While that may be true, many people owe a great deal to him. Some he has taught how to thrive under pressure and fulfill a collective purpose as one. Others he has provided entertainment, inspiration, and a model of leadership. And some he has given a great opponent to measure their achievements against. What we owe Mike Krzyzewski is admiration, grudging or otherwise, for winning in a way that offers lessons for us all.

CHRONOLOGY

1947 Michael William Krzyzewski is born in Chicago.

1969 Mike weds Mickie Marsh and graduates from West Point.

1980 Krzyzewski becomes Duke's head basketball coach.

1984 A 77–75 triumph over North Carolina gives Coach K his first victory over a top-ranked team and his first trip to the ACC Tournament title game.

1985 Krzyzewski notches his first win in the NCAA Tournament, beating Pepperdine 75–62.

1986 With a 71–67 win over Kansas, Duke wins thirty-seven games in a season, setting an NCAA record and sending Krzyzewski to his first national championship game.

1988 Duke upsets No. 1 seed Temple 63–53 to send Coach K to his second Final Four.

1990 The Blue Devils top Connecticut 79–78 on a buzzer-beater by Christian Laettner, making Duke the seventh school to make it to the Final Four three years in a row.

1991 Duke upsets unbeaten UNLV, 79–77, to advance to the NCAA championship. Coach K's squad beats Kansas for his first national title.

1992 Duke defeats Michigan 71–51 to repeat as national champions.

1992 Krzyzewski serves as assistant coach to Chuck Daly on the US Olympic squad known as the "Dream Team" in Barcelona, where they take home the gold medal.

1994 The Arkansas Razorbacks deny Duke its third championship in four years with a 76–72 victory in the NCAA title game.

1999 Connecticut stuns Duke, 77–74, in the national championship game.

2001 Duke topples Arizona to make Krzyzewski the fourth men's Division I coach to win three NCAA championships.

2001 Coach K is voted into the Naismith Memorial Basketball Hall of Fame in his very first year of eligibility.

2008 With Krzyzewski in command, Team USA wins a gold medal at the 2008 Beijing Summer Olympics with a 118–107 victory over Spain.

2010 Coach K claims his fourth national championship with Duke's 61–59 win over Butler.

2011 Duke outlasts Michigan State, 74–69, at Madison Square Garden to give their coach his 903rd career win, an NCAA record.

2012 Krzyzewski directs Team USA to a 107–100 win over Spain to claim the gold medal at the London Olympics.

2015 The Blue Devils beat Wisconsin by a 68–63 score to secure Coach K's fifth NCAA title. Only John Wooden won more championships as an NCAA men's basketball coach.

2015 Krzyzewski sets a record as the first Division I men's basketball coach to claim 1,000 wins in his career.

2016 Coach K concludes his tenure as the US Olympic coach with a gold medal at the Summer Games in Rio de Janeiro.

CHAPTER NOTES

INTRODUCTION

1. Mike Krzyzewski and Donald T. Phillips, *Five-Point Play: Duke's Journey to the 2001 National Championship* (New York, NY: Warner Books, 2001), p. xi.
2. Eric Prisbell, "Players, colleagues praise Mike Krzyzewski's ability to connect, adapt, win," USA Today, March 31, 2015, https://www.usatoday.com/story/sports/ncaab/2015/03/31/mike-krzyewski-duke-blue-devins-final-four/70737542/.
3. Ibid.
4. John Feinstein and Mike Krzyzewski. *Last Dance: Behind the Scenes at the Final Four* (Boston, MA: Back Bay Books, 2007), p. 252.
5. Mike Krzyzewski and Donald T. Phillips, *Leading with the Heart: Coach K's Successful Strategies for Basketball, Business, and Life* (New York, NY: Warner Books, 2000), p. 117.
6. Ibid., p. 6.
7. Mike Krzyzewski and Jamie K. Spatola, *Beyond Basketball: Coach K's Keywords for Success* (New York, NY: Warner Business Books, 2006), p. 158.
8. Ibid., p. 27.

9. Barry Jacobs, *Coach K's Little Blue Book: Lessons From College Basketball's Best Coach* (Kingston, NY: Total Sports Publishing, 2000) p. 88.
10. Alexander Wolff, "Blue Angel," *Sports Illustrated*, March 16, 1992, https://www.si.com/vault/1992/03/16/126154/blue-angel-duke-coach-mike-krzyzewskis-divine-spirit-and-working-class-ethics-have-forged-an-exemplary-college-basketball-program.

CHAPTER 1. WORKING-CLASS ORIGINS AND ARMY DISCIPLINE

1. Mike Krzyzewski and Jamie K. Spatola, *Beyond Basketball: Coach K's Keywords for Success* (New York, NY: Warner Business Books, 2006), p. 141.
2. Ibid., p. 122.
3. Ibid., p. 92.
4. Ibid., p. 93.
5. Ibid., p. 89.
6. Ibid., p. 135.
7. Mike Krzyzewski and Donald T. Phillips, *Leading with the Heart: Coach K's Successful Strategies for Basketball, Business, and Life* (New York, NY: Warner Books, 2000), p. 37.
8. Krzyzewski and Spatola, *Beyond Basketball: Coach K's Keywords for Success*, p. 66.
9. Krzyzewski and Phillips, p. 45.
10. Barry Jacobs, *Coach K's Little Blue Book: Lessons from College Basketball's Best Coach* (Kingston, NY: Total Sports Publishing, 2000), p. 14.
11. Wolff, Alexander, "Blue Angel," *Sports Illustrated,* March 16, 1992, https://www.si.com/vault/1992/03/16/126154/.

blue-angel-duke-coach-mike-krzyzewskis-divine-spirit-and-working-class-ethics-have-forged-an-exemplary-college-basketball-program.

CHAPTER 2. SPECIAL K

1. Mike Krzyzewski and Donald T. Phillips, *Leading with the Heart: Coach K's Successful Strategies for Basketball, Business, and Life* (New York, NY: Warner Books, 2000), p. 62.
2. Mike Krzyzewski and Jamie K. Spatola, *Beyond Basketball: Coach K's Keywords for Success* (New York, NY: Warner Business Books, 2006), p. 122.
3. Ibid., p. 70.
4. Ibid., p. 14.
5. Ibid., p. 65.
6. Krzyzewski and Phillips, p. 57.
7. John Feinstein and Mike Krzyzewski. *Last Dance: Behind the Scenes at the Final Four* (Boston, MA: Back Bay Books, 2007), p. 7.
8. Barry Jacobs, *Coach K's Little Blue Book: Lessons from College Basketball's Best Coach* (Kingston, NY: Total Sports Publishing, 2000), p. 15.
9. Feinstein and Krzyzewski, p. 97.
10. Jacobs, p. 16.
11. John Feinstein, *The Legends Club* (New York, NY: Doubleday, 2016), p. 46.
12. Feinstein and Krzyzewski, p. 98.
13. Jacobs, p. 16.
14. Feinstein and Krzyzewski, p. 8.
15. Krzyzewski and Spatola, p. 85.
16. Krzyzewski and Phillips, p. 75.
17. Feinstein and Krzyzewski, p. 9.
18. Ibid., p. 10.

CHAPTER 3. CLOSING IN ON A CHAMPIONSHIP, ONE STEP AT A TIME

1. Mike Krzyzewski and Jamie K. Spatola, *Beyond Basketball: Coach K's Keywords for Success* (New York, NY: Warner Business Books, 2006), p. 31.
2. Mike Krzyzewski and Donald T. Phillips, *Leading with the Heart: Coach K's Successful Strategies for Basketball, Business, and Life* (New York, NY: Warner Books, 2000), p. 26.
3. Ibid., p. 103.
4. Krzyzewski and Spatola, p. 40.
5. Barry Jacobs, *Coach K's Little Blue Book: Lessons from College Basketball's Best Coach* (Kingston, NY: Total Sports Publishing, 2000), p. 66.
6. Wolff, Alexander, "Blue Angel," *Sports Illustrated*, March 16, 1992, https://www.si.com/vault/1992/03/16/126154/blue-angel-duke-coach-mike krzyzewskis divine spirit and working class ethics have forged an-exemplary-college-basketball-program.
7. Krzyzewski and Spatola, p. 26.
8. John Feinstein, *A March to Madness* (New York, NY: Little, Brown and Company, 1998) p. 47.
9. Ibid., p. 64.
10. John Feinstein and Mike Krzyzewski. *Last Dance: Behind the Scenes at the Final Four* (Boston, MA: Back Bay Books, 2007), p.18.
11. Krzyzewski and Phillips, p. 168.
12. Ibid.
13. Ibid., p. 59.
14. Ibid., p. 27.
15. Ibid., p. 19.
16. Feinstein, p. 64.

17. Krzyzewski and Phillips, p. 177.
18. Ibid., p. 32.
19. Krzyzewski and Spatola, p. 41.
20. Krzyzewski and Phillips, p. 178.
21. Ibid., p. 182.

CHAPTER 4. DUKE DID IT AGAIN

1. Mike Krzyzewski and Donald T. Phillips, *Leading with the Heart: Coach K's Successful Strategies for Basketball, Business, and Life* (New York, NY: Warner Books, 2000), p. 28.
2. Barry Jacobs, *Coach K's Little Blue Book: Lessons from College Basketball's Best Coach* (Kingston, NY: Total Sports Publishing, 2000), p. 29.
3. Krzyzewski and Phillips, p. 173.
4. John Feinstein and Mike Krzyzewski. *Last Dance: Behind the Scenes at the Final Four* (Boston, MA: Back Bay Books, 2007), p. 10.
5. Krzyzewski and Phillips, p. 138.
6. Jacobs, p. 41.
7. Krzyzewski and Phillips, p. 140.
8. Ibid., p. 210.
9. Ibid., p. 161.
10. Mike Krzyzewski and Jamie K. Spatola, *Beyond Basketball: Coach K's Keywords for Success* (New York, NY: Warner Business Books, 2006), p. 47.
11. Krzyzewski and Phillips, p. 163.
12. Alexander Wolff, "The Man Couldn't Miss," *Sports Illustrated*, April 6, 1992, https://www.si.com/vault/1992/04/06/126296/ncaa-east-the-man-couldnt-miss-christian-laettners-perfect-shooting-propelled-duke-to-its-fifth-consecutive-final-four.
13. Krzyzewski and Phillips, p. 164.

14. Lucy McCalmont, "Over 20 Years Later, Christian Laettner Apologizes to Aminu Timberlake for Stomping on Him," *Huffington Post,* March 16, 2015, https://www.huffingtonpost.com/2015/03/16/christian-laettner-apology-stomp_n_6877014.html.
15. Jacobs, p. 84.
16. Krzyzewski and Phillips, p. 128.

CHAPTER 5. THE UNDOING OF A DELICATE DYNASTY

1. Barry Jacobs, *Coach K's Little Blue Book: Lessons from College Basketball's Best Coach* (Kingston, NY: Total Sports Publishing, 2000), p. 24.
2. Mike Krzyzewski and Jamie K. Spatola, *Beyond Basketball: Coach K's Keywords for Success* (New York, NY: Warner Business Books, 2006), p. 38.
3. Thomas George, "Cal Repels Comeback and Dethrones Duke," *New York Times*, March 21, 1993, http://www.nytimes.com/1993/03/21/sports/ncaa-tournament-midwest-cal-repels-comeback-and-dethrones-duke.html.
4. Jacobs, p. 78.
5. Mike Krzyzewski and Donald T. Phillips, *Leading with the Heart: Coach K's Successful Strategies for Basketball, Business, and Life* (New York, NY: Warner Books, 2000), p. 131.
6. Steve Berkowitz, "Arkansas Hits Hog Heaven with NCAA Title," *Washington Post*, April 5, 1994, http://www.washingtonpost.com/wp-srv/sports/longterm/memories/final4/articles/final94.htm.
7. John Feinstein, *A March to Madness* (New York, NY: Little, Brown and Company, 1998), p. 68.
8. Krzyzewski and Phillips, p. 272.
9. Jacobs, p. 20.
10. Feinstein, p. 70.
11. Krzyzewski and Phillips, p. 274.

12. Ibid., p. 275.
13. Ibid., p. 221.
14. Krzyzewski and Spatola, p. 60.
15. Feinstein, p. 429.

CHAPTER 6. DEVILISHLY CLEVER

1. Mike Krzyzewski and Jamie K. Spatola, *Beyond Basketball: Coach K's Keywords for Success* (New York, NY: Warner Business Books, 2006), p. 20.
2. John Feinstein, *The Legends Club* (New York, NY: Doubleday, 2016), p. 339.
3. Joe Drape, "UConn Upsets Duke to Grab NCAA Title," *New York Times*, March 30, 1999, http://www.nytimes.com/1999/03/30/sports/ncaa tournament-uconn-upsets-duke-to-grab-ncaa-title.html
4. Judy Battista, "Langdon's Journey Is a Step Too Long," *New York Times,* March 30, 1999, http://www.nytimes.com/1999/03/30/sports/ncaa-tournament-men-s-championship-langdon-s-journey-is-a-step-too-long.html
5. John Feinstein and Mike Krzyzewski. *Last Dance: Behind the Scenes at the Final Four* (Boston, MA: Back Bay Books, 2007), pg. 12.
6. Mike Krzyzewski and Donald T. Phillips, *Five-Point Play: Duke's Journey to the 2001 National Championship* (New York, NY: Warner Books, 2001), p. 2.
7. Mike Krzyzewski and Jamie K. Spatola, p. 21.
8. Ibid., p. 21.
9. Ibid., p. 22.
10. Barry Jacobs, *Coach K's Little Blue Book: Lessons from College Basketball's Best Coach* (Kingston, NY: Total Sports Publishing, 2000), p. 95.
11. Krzyzewski and Phillips, p. xi.
12. Ibid., p. 107.
13. Krzyzewski and Spatola, p. 15.

14. Krzyzewski and Phillips, p. 133.
15. Ibid., p. 144.
16. Ibid., p. 146.
17. Ibid., p. 222.
18. Krzyzewski and Spatola, p. 96.

CHAPTER 7. COULD THE COUNTRY STILL COMPETE?

1. Mike Krzyzewski and Jamie K. Spatola, *Beyond Basketball: Coach K's Keywords for Success* (New York, NY: Warner Business Books, 2006), p. 24.
2. Mike Krzyzewski and Jamie K. Spatola, *The Gold Standard: Building a World-Class Team* (New York, NY: Business Plus, 2009), p. 136.
3. Ibid., p. 23.
4. Ibid., p. 147.
5. Ibid., p. 69.
6. Ibid., p. 33.
7. Ibid., p. 59.
8. Ibid., p. 71.
9. Ibid., p. 98.
10. Ibid., p. 183.
11. Krzyzewski and Spatola, *Beyond Basketball*, p. 130.
12. Krzyzewski and Spatola, *The Gold Standard*, p. 218.

CHAPTER 8. A COACH WHO REALLY CARES

1. Mike Krzyzewski and Jamie K. Spatola, *Beyond Basketball: Coach K's Keywords for Success* (New York, NY: Warner Business Books, 2006), p. 88.
2. Ibid., p. 93.

3. Mike Krzyzewski and Donald T. Phillips, *Leading with the Heart: Coach K's Successful Strategies for Basketball, Business, and Life* (New York, NY: Warner Books, 2000), p. 269.
4. Ibid., p. 270.
5. Ibid., p. 8.
6. Krzyzewski and Spatola, p. 86.
7. Ibid., p. 49.
8. Ibid., p. 20.
9. Ibid., p. 137.
10. Alexander Wolff, "Blue Angel," *Sports Illustrated*, March 16, 1992,https://www.si.com/vault/1992/03/16/126154/blue-angel-duke-coach-mike-krzyzewskis-divine-spirit-and-working-class-ethics-have-forged-an-exemplary-college-basketball-program.
11. Krzyzewski and Spatola, p. 78.
12. Ibid., p. 112.
13. Ibid., p. 83.

CHAPTER 9. KRZYZEWSKI IS ONE OF A KIND

1. Mike Kline, "Mike Krzyzewski's 20 Best Quotes from His Time as Duke's Coach," *Bleacher Report*, March 1, 2011, http://bleacherreport.com/articles/623308-mike-krzyzewskis-20-best-quotes-from-his-time-as-dukes-coach.
2. Mike Krzyzewski and Jamie K. Spatola, *Beyond Basketball: Coach K's Keywords for Success* (New York, NY: Warner Business Books, 2006), p. 155.
3. John Feinstein, *The Legends Club* (New York, NY: Doubleday, 2016), p. 362.
4. Ibid., p. 446.
5. Ibid., p. 372.
6. Ibid., p. 375.

7. Ibid., p. 375.
8. Luke Decock, "For Coach K, Olympic Mission Now Complete," *The News & Observer*, August 22, 2016, http://www.newsobserver.com/sports/spt-columns-blogs/luke-decock/article97055187.html#storylink=cpy.
9. Mike Krzyzewski and Donald T. Phillips, *Leading with the Heart: Coach K's Successful Strategies for Basketball, Business, and Life* (New York, NY: Warner Books, 2000), p. 221.
10. Feinstein, p. Acknowledgements.
11. Barry Jacobs, *Coach K's Little Blue Book: Lessons from College Basketball's Best Coach* (Kingston, NY: Total Sports Publishing, 2000), p. 46.
12. Daniels, Evan, "Mike Krzyzewski on Marvin Bagley: 'He's Got a Big Future,'" 247 Sports, November 8, 2017, https://247sports.com/Article/Mike-Krzyzewski-on-Marvin-Bagley-Hes-got-a-big-future-110162669.
13. Krzyzewski and Phillips, p. 273.
14. Jacobs, p. 102.
15. Ibid., p. 123.

GLOSSARY

Cinderella team Competitors who achieve far greater postseason success than expected.

Division I The highest level of intercollegiate athletics sanctioned by the NCAA.

field goal A basket scored on any shot other than a free throw. Field goals can be worth two or three points depending on the shooter's distance from the basket.

Final Four The national semifinals of the NCAA Tournament, when only four teams remain in contention for the championship.

full-court press When the defense applies pressure to the offense the entire length of the court, before and after the inbound pass.

inbound pass When a player on the sideline tries to put the ball in play by passing it to a teammate on the court.

NCAA Short for National Collegiate Athletic Association, the governing body for college sports.

"one-and-one" A type of foul shot, beginning with the seventh foul of a half, when one free throw is awarded per foul. If the player makes the first free throw, he gets to shoot one more.

point guard The position generally responsible for running the offense and distributing the ball to teammates on the offensive side of the court.

plebe A newly entered cadet or freshman, especially at a military academy.

rebound The statistic associated with securing a missed shot after the ball hits the rim of the basket.

roster The list of players on a team and available to play in a game.

screen When a player stops moving in position to block a defender from following her teammate.

seed In a tournament, the ranking that determines who a team or competitor plays first. Typically, the purpose of seeding is to separate favorites to win the tournament for as long as possible.

turnover When a player loses possession of the ball to the other team.

two-guard Also known as the shooting guard or "two," this player is more concerned with scoring than distributing the ball to teammates.

zone A form of defense where a player guards an area, not another player.

FURTHER READING

BOOKS

Davis, Seth. *Getting to Us: How Great Coaches Make Great Teams.* New York, NY: Penguin Press, 2018.

Krzyzewski, Mike, and Donald T. Phillips. *Leading with the Heart: Coach K's Successful Strategies for Basketball, Business, and Life.* New York, NY: Warner Books, 2000.

Krzyzewski, Mike, and Donald T. Phillips. *Five-Point Play: Duke's Journey to the 2001 National Championship.* New York, NY: Warner Books, 2001.

Krzyzewski, Mike, and Jamie K. Spatola. *Beyond Basketball: Coach K's Keywords for Success.* New York, NY: Warner Books, 2006.

Krzyzewski, Mike, and Jamie K. Spatola. *The Gold Standard: Building a World-Class Team*. Business Plus, 2009.

WEBSITES

Coach K.com

coachk.com

The official site of Mike Krzyzewski.

Duke Basketball

www.goduke.com

Get an inside look at the Blue Devils, with interviews, news, stats, game previews, and more.

FILMS

Duke '91 & '92: Back to Back. TNT, 2012.

Duke-Carolina: The Blue Blood Rivalry. Image Entertainment, 2013.

INDEX

L

M

N

O

P

R

S

T

U

V

W

Z